Be Prepared! An Effective Disaster Management Plan

Ways to Prepare for Every Kind of Disaster

Robert Reinoehl

PUBLISHED BY:
Robert Reinoehl
Copyright © 2012

Disclaimer
The information contained in this book is for general information purposes only. The information is provided by the authors and while we endeavor to keep the information up to date and correct, we make no representations or warranties of any kind, express or implied, about the completeness, accuracy, reliability, suitability or availability with respect to the book or the information, products, services, or related graphics contained in the book for any purpose. Any reliance you place on such information is therefore strictly at your own risk.

TABLE OF CONTENTS

Part I: Introduction to Disaster Preparedness

Chapter 1: What is a Disaster?

What is a disaster?

A disaster is an unexpected event that causes destruction. Disasters cause loss – of life, of property, of money, and of happiness. They strike at any time and any place. They can take away your home and your family. Some disasters are natural, and some are caused by humans.

This report will explore the different types of disasters that can happen to you and your family. It will tell you what you can do to prepare for a disaster, and how to survive during one. It will explain how to secure primary needs like food, water, and shelter. It will also cover secondary needs like communication, electricity, and finances. It will cover evacuation plans and survival kits.

Although one report could never contain exhaustive information on the topic of disaster survival, this quick reference will allow you to get through almost any catastrophe.

Why should I be prepared for a disaster?

We live in an age when a person in New York can travel to meet another one in Sydney in a little over a day. Through the internet, those same two people could communicate in seconds. In this age, where every want and every need is at our fingertips, it may seem odd or old-fashioned to prepare for a disaster.

However, disasters wipe out roads and lines of communication. They make essential needs scarce and difficult to obtain, and they hit people unaware. Once a disaster strikes, there will be no chance to look on the Internet or even go to the library to learn how to deal with it.

Whether it is a fire in your own home, an earthquake from a distant epicenter, or a terrorist taking hostages, it is imperative people are prepared to deal with disasters before they come.

How can you be prepared for unknown disasters?

Although disasters are unpredictable, the consequences of any disaster are not. Every disaster follows predictable patterns. By observing the patterns of previous disasters, you can learn how to deal with a future disaster before it strikes.

Few parents plan the birth of their first child. However, there are signs that a baby is on the way – the woman grows larger; she feels sick; she has to use the restroom constantly. They have no idea when they will get to see their child, but they know one day it will come. By the time the baby enters the world, the parents have prepared for it. They have clothing, a bed, and blankets. Even though they never have experienced what caring for a baby is like, they have learned what they need from others who know about baby care. Then with that knowledge they prepared for the baby.

People can also prepare for a disaster. By learning how to prepare and what to do before the disaster strikes, you will be more level headed and able to deal with whatever catastrophe comes your way. By preparing your family, you will be able to work together as a unit and overcome any difficulties.

Chapter 2: Overview: Types of Disasters

Natural Disasters

A natural disaster is a destructive event caused by nature. Natural disasters occur less frequently than other disasters. However, humans have no control over these disasters and little or no warning of when they are going to occur. In the past fifteen years, natural disasters have been responsible for more than one million people dead and more than three million people homeless.

Although they occur relatively infrequently, natural disasters affect large areas which increase their death toll. Of all natural disasters, earthquakes and tsunamis are by far the deadliest. Floods (and hurricanes) would be a close second. All four of these natural disasters can lead to a loss of home and possessions as well as loss of life.

Examples of Natural Disasters

Natural disasters include:

- Heat waves
- Blizzards
- Earthquakes
- Volcanoes
- Tsunamis
- Solar Flares
- Wildfires
- Floods
- Hurricanes
- Tornados, cyclones, and twisters

Pandemic

A pandemic is a disease that has gone beyond local containment and spread to a large geographic area. Prior to the 1920's, pandemics were common and occurred in relatively predictable cycles. The last flu pandemic killed more than 20 million people worldwide. However, the invention of modern medicine and the ability to mass produce antibiotics, such as penicillin, caused the threat of pandemic to fade in the minds of most people.

With new diseases being discovered and antibiotic resistance spreading, the risk of a modern pandemic is very real. In our modern world, sick people are encouraged to go to work, and work spaces are often crowded and poorly ventilated. In addition, the world is interconnected. A person can fly halfway around the world in about one day, stopping at several airports to spread any diseases they may be carrying.

Add to the mix that diseases considered eradicated, such as smallpox, have been sequenced genetically, posted on the internet, and recreated in laboratory settings.

Examples of Pandemics

Some possible pandemics include:

- Influenza
- SARS
- Ebola
- Polio
- Smallpox

Manmade Disasters

Unlike natural disasters, manmade disasters are usually caused when people make mistakes. They happen rather frequently, but usually few human lives are lost. Like natural disasters, there is little warning before they occur. Some of them, such as power outages, are not deadly in and of themselves, but all of them can kill if people are unprepared for them.

Examples of Manmade Disasters

Some man-made disasters are:

- Hazardous material spills
- Power outages
- House fires
- HEMPs
- Nuclear Meltdowns
- Economic Meltdown

Acts of Violence

As long as societies have existed, people have committed acts of violence against other people. Whether an all out war with one nation or a group of nations against another, or an individual attack performed as a demonstration of an ideal, these violent outbursts on society often seem senseless.

Although the UN and other overseeing bodies attempt to limit the number of these acts, it seems like the more information that passes rapidly through society, the more hatred and violence pass with it.

Examples of Acts of Violence

Acts of violence include:

- Biological and chemical threats
- Terrorism
- Cyber attacks

Personal Disasters

Personal disasters can sometimes be predicted, but they only affect one person and perhaps his or her family. An illness such as cancer that is not communicable, the loss of a job, or perhaps a car accident can cause abnormal stress on a person that can last for weeks or even years. Planning for personal emergencies is a part of any disaster planning. Obtaining personal documents such as living wills and car insurance are just as valuable as obtaining food stores.

Personal disasters are usually the easiest to prepare for with minimal effort, but few people choose to have the foresight to prepare for them. When the personal disaster arises, the unprepared person experience more stress and causes more strain on their immediate family than the prepared person.

Chapter 3: Disaster Preparedness

Where do I begin?

To begin to prepare for a disaster, you should first assess which disasters can befall you. If you live in a desert, you chances of encountering a blizzard are low. Planning for a blizzard and not planning for a heat wave would be foolish. Look at the disasters covered in this report and determine which ones are most likely to befall you. Then take steps to protect yourself from them.

After deciding which disasters may befall you, create a list that includes what you need to survive each, and cross off the needs you can already meet. For example, if you have a garden and can preserve food, you probably will have well stocked cupboards. However, you may not have access to the abundance of potable water; you will need to keep your garden growing after a disaster. After you discover which needs you can meet and which you cannot, you can begin to organize the items you have in a logical manner and stock supplies you do not have.

I panic in a disaster. What is the most important thing for me to remember?

The most noteworthy thing to remember is to Assess the Scene and Keep away from harm (ASK). Whenever a disaster occurs, look around and find the safest place to take shelter. That is the place you want to be. You can prepare yourself for disasters by making a habit of assessing scenes. When you go to your brother's wedding, for example, look around and think about where the safest place would be in an earthquake. By constantly evaluating scenes, you will become quicker at finding the safest place in any emergency. If a disaster occurs, you will already know the safest place to be and shave vital seconds from the time it will take you to get there.

How do I create a disaster plan for my family?

To create a disaster plan for your family, make a list of your family neighborhood meeting place, your local meeting place, and your out-of-town meeting place. List phone numbers of out-of-state contact people. List all the members of your family, their dates of birth, and pertinent medical information about them, including any medicines they take.

Next, list all the places where your family members spend time and the phone numbers and addresses of the places. Schools, places of employment, health clubs, and churches should all be on here if you regularly go to them. If you know the evacuation spot of the places of business, list that as well. Add a list of your insurance policies and the contact information for the insurance company associated with the policy.

Post your disaster plan by a telephone with a notebook and two pens. Make abridged copies on note cards with in-town and out-of-town emergency contact names and phone numbers, your local and out-of-town meeting places, and your medical information. Have each member of your family carry these copies on him or her at all times.

Does my family need specific training to deal with a disaster?

Anyone can cope with a short term disaster without special training. In a power outage, for example, there is no need for a family to do anything other than turn on a flashlight and a battery operated alarm clock. If the outage occurs before bedtime one night and is remedied by morning, there will be little disruption to your family life. However, with extensive emergencies like an EMP, training can save the life of you and your family.

Training takes time, effort, and often money to complete. Everything you invest into learning new survival skills will be returned the first time you must use them. Some relevant disaster skills are: community first aid and CPR, firearm safety and target practice, instruction in using edible plants and herbs, gardening, wilderness survival, electric circuits, plumbing, and carpentry. Frequently, you can find basic courses on a variety of topics at colleges and community centers.

Training, like supplies, should be checked for necessity. If you live in the country, learning how to grow your own food may be more valuable than learning how to protect your home. A basic course in first aid will always be more pertinent than learning how to perform a tracheostomy (where you cut a hole in someone's throat to help them breath). Learning how to subjugate a potential looter with your bare hands should not be placed over learning how to use a firearm or weapon. Once you have a list of necessary skills you and your family should learn, set to learning them one at a time, so you can learn them well. Also, do not attempt to perform risky tasks that you have not received training to do. A certified electrician might be able to rewire you house to run off homemade solar cells, but this is not a job for the armchair handyman.

What is a family meeting place?

Some people live alone in a city with no relatives. They can skip this section unless they want to use the idea for close friends.

Every family should have a family neighborhood meeting place. If you live with your family, this place should be a safe place somewhere outside your home. To keep a family meeting place safe, it should be away from trees and buildings, and it should not be located in the street or in another dangerous place.

If you do not live in the same household but live in the same city as the rest of your family, you can inform them of your local meeting place. A local meeting place is at a centralized location that several families or family members scattered across the city could meet if a disaster strikes. Choose a family meeting place in a central location that is easy for other friends and family to reach. Again, this place must be safe, but you should also choose a place with a familiar landmark that could be identified even in the event of massive destruction. Everyone who is going to be using the family meeting place needs to know where it is. It is an excellent idea to have "drills" once or twice a year where the entire family meets in this place. The purpose is for the family to stay in the meeting place until everyone is there or a fireman or policeman tells you to leave (for example if the area has become unsafe). If the latter is the case, someone should leave a note under a rock for any family members not present. The note should inform absent family members where to find the others.

Finally, you need to have an out-of-town meeting place. This is a place to which you can flee if you need to evacuate. It should be a minimum of fifty miles away from your home town. It can be a relative's home or a motel that accepts pets and sits across the street from a storage rental area.

Basic survival kit

Making a basic survival kit is the first step to being prepared for any disaster. It should be placed in a small bag or preferably a backpack. Gather all the items and check them once a month. Rotate the older food and water items out of the kit and put new items into it. Check to make sure everything, such as the flashlight, is working properly and fix or replace items that are not. The basic survival kit should help you get through 72-hours of any disaster. It should be portable, and able to be individualized if more than one person will be using it. Other names for a basic survival kit are: "72-hour kit," "grab bag," "GOOD bag" (Get Out Of Dodge), "PERK" (Personal Emergency Relocation Kit), or "go bag."

Include these items in your personal basic survival kit (or Bug-Out Bag):

- First aid kit (described later)
- Iodine or chlorine water purification kits
- Measuring spoons and 1 cup size plastic measuring cup
- Energy bars to give 7,500 calories (3 days worth of calories)
- Light weight rain poncho
- Folding shovel
- Lightweight tent.
- Pocketknife with saw tooth option
- Flashlight and batteries (or crank)

- Butane lighter
- Lip balm and hard candy
- Toilet paper
- Package of sanitary items for women
- Hand crank radio (or radio with batteries)
- Charged cell phone
- Five day supply of any prescription medicines
- Roll of pennies, dimes, nickels, and quarters, $20 in dollar coins, $20 in ones, and $40 in fives
- Three day supply of socks and underwear
- Can opener
- Travel bottle of dish soap
- Hand sanitizer
- Pen and small notebook
- Maps with evacuation routes marked
- Travel toothbrush and toothpaste
- Whistle/ three signal flares
- 3 gallons water
- 4 rolls duct tape
- Sleeping bag and bed roll (your pack can act as a pillow or use a camp pillow)
- Weapons (if you are not going to a shelter – if you are, bring walking sticks)
- Compass (learn how to use it before a disaster)

If you have children, be sure to include a book, coloring book, or some other entertainment. Minimalist campers and backpackers can survive for days on less, but this is the minimum recommended for a family. Dress for the worst weather you expect, you will be wearing these clothes until you reach your destination, whether that is a safe room in your own home or a relative's home several states away.

What priorities should I take care of first when a disaster hits?

The first thing to take care of in any disaster is the safety of you and your family. Make sure you are in the safest place possible to survive until the actual disaster has passed. Step two is to provide first aid to anyone in need of it. Step three is to secure your primary needs. Step four is to provide secondary needs and determine when, if ever, you should evacuate the area.

Chapter 4: Children and Disaster Management

How do I teach my children about disasters without scaring them?

The easiest way to teach children about disasters is to turn practicing for them into a game. Take a community CPR and First Aid class together. Take a firearms safety course together.

Here are some examples of survival games you can play with children:

- 911: Randomly call out emergencies and non-emergencies. The child tells whether or not they should call 911, and then gives their full name, address, phone number and a description of the emergency. (This could be played in the car.)

- Emergency Hospital: Get out a practice first aid kit (one that you would not use in a real emergency but you can use to practice with repeatedly). Have the child practice healing you from different ailments using first aid. Gather several stuffed animals and dolls to create an entire hospital.

- Weekend non-emergency. Practice living without power for the weekend by camping out in your backyard. Purchase what you will use of your emergency food supply and use the older supplies to help rotate stock.

- It is also a very good idea to randomly "check" your fire alarm. Every time your children hear it, they should stop what they are doing and leave the house. You can pretend to be a fire they cannot get past so they can practice an alternate route. All your children should meet at the family meeting place and stay there until you come to tell them that it is safe to return to the house.

What do my children need to know if they are separated from me in a disaster?

Whenever you are in any public place, whether during a disaster or not, if you and your child(ren) become separated, the child should automatically stop as soon as they realize they are split apart from you. If the child is in an unsafe place such as the street, he or she should retrace his or her steps to the nearest safe place.

Although it is usually best to remain in one place during a disaster, there are times when it is necessary to move through a disaster zone. When a child loses his or her adult, it is the adult's responsibility to go back and find the child. It is never advisable for a child to try to move through a disaster zone unchaperoned.

What can children do if an emergency or disaster occurs when they are alone?

If your child is staying alone or is out by themselves when a disaster occurs, it is important for him or her to know the rules of surviving during a disaster. They should immediately go to the safest place available until the disaster is finished.

After the immediate danger of the disaster has passed, the child needs to know when to stay put (if they are in a place their parents will expect to find them, and it is safe) and when to go to the agreed upon meeting place. If the child needs to go to the meeting place, he or she should take his or her basic supply kit along if possible and leave a note visibly under a rock that has the child's initials, the day and time, and the words "Local Safe Place," or "Neighborhood Safe Place" depending on where the child is going. They should not write their full names or exact directions. After the immediate danger of the disaster has passed, it is the adult's responsibility to find the child by cycling through the most obvious places. For this reason, it is imperative that you always know where you child is. If the child is at home alone, the adult must make every effort to return to their home. If your child is at a friend's home, check there first.

Whenever parents and children are separated during disaster, it can be scary for both. However, if the child(ren) follows the family disaster plan, leaves notes when relocating, and tries to remain in one place, he or she will be easier to locate.

72-hour Baby Evacuation Kit

Babies have special needs that must be prepared for in the event of an emergency. If you are the parent or guardian of an infant or child under the age of two, here are some things you should include in a survival kit for them:

- Disposable diapers and wipes
- Two plastic garbage bags (one for soiled diapers, one for soiled clothing)
- Four extra changes of clothes and two blankets
- Moist towelettes
- Diaper rash ointment and suntan lotion with an SPF of 30 or higher
- Bottle with disposable liners and extra liners
- Medication – including baby acetaminophen, baby ibuprofen, baby Vicks, and baby pseudoephedrine type product.
- Baby food
- Formula
- Three gallons bottle water

Keep in mind that if you have to travel with a baby, plan frequent breaks and make sure the infant stays hydrated. If you are on the go, bury used diapers. If not, you can keep them in a plastic garbage bag. Also, purchase a baby carrier that works as a front pack so you can carry a backpack and the child at the same time.

Chapter 5: Special Needs: Disaster Management for Seniors and the Disabled

I am older and disabled. I live by myself. What will happen to me if I am injured in a disaster?

If you are elderly, disabled, or both, the best way to survive a disaster is by preparing in advance. During a disaster, your chances of becoming injured are greater than those who do not have special needs. Inform emergency departments that you are have special needs and you live alone. Make sure you have a younger neighbor or family member who lives nearby with a key who is willing to check on you. It is also a good idea to install an emergency alert system in your home. Medical alert devices that you can wear around your neck and can signal help are very useful in the case of a disaster emergency.

What can an older or disabled person do to prepare for a disaster?

People with special needs should stock food and water like any other person. Keeping a basic survival kit on hand is an excellent idea. Those who are older or disabled need to keep a folder in a convenient place that contains all the information about your medical needs that includes medicines you take, conditions you have, allergy information, all you medical devices, doctors, and emergency contacts.

Is there special equipment a disabled or older person may need to survive a disaster?

If you rely on equipment that requires electricity, make sure your power company is aware of your need. Investing in a generator is an excellent idea as well. Even if you do not need electrical equipment, the generator can be used to run an electric heater/air conditioner to protect you from weather extremes.

People with respiratory problems will not be able to use face masks, gas masks, or several protective coverings. If you have respiratory problems, you will need to purchase a SCBA in order to protect yourself in the case of a chemical/ biological/ or radiation disaster.

Consider buying your prescription medicines in three to four month supplies. This will ensure you have some on hand for long term events. Also, if you use special devices like wheelchairs or walking sticks, stock extras in the trunk of your car or a closet near the front door.

Chapter 6: Preparing for a Disaster Financially

Insurance – the best disaster plan

People who live with no insurance or not enough insurance are just borrowing time until they have a serious accident, which causes them to lose everything. At the least, you should have insurance on your house and its contents or renter's insurance. These two types of insurance protect everything you own. In case all your possessions are destroyed, properly insuring them will allow you to get them back with minimal expense. Be sure to take "before" pictures of you most valuable and costly items.

Auto insurance is another notable type of insurance everyone should carry. One accident can cause financial destruction if you have no insurance to help recover losses. Even if your car is worth very little, medical bills can become extraordinary.

Life insurance and disability insurance can protect the rest of the family if one of the members is lost. An effective amount of life insurance will cover not only funeral costs, but provide enough money to pay off all your outstanding debts. It should also provide enough money to replace the income of the person who has died.

Long-term disability insurance is a must for anyone over the age of 50. Long-term disability insurance pays for nursing home care so that you do not have to liquidate your estate if you need this. The sooner you acquire this insurance, the lower your payments will be.

Emergency savings

An emergency fund is a liquid (accessible money, as opposed to money tied in a CD or stocks) monetary buffer to be used in case of emergency. This money should only be used for true emergencies. Ideally, you should have three months worth of income saved in your emergency savings fund.

Precious metals

There are several ways to purchase precious metals such as gold, but not all of them are useful in case of disaster. The easiest way to purchase gold is on the stock exchange. If you buy gold this way, you will never see it; it is stored in a bank. Your chances of making money off gold purchased as an investment are equal to your chance of making money on any other stock. No one can predict bull or bear markets nor can they predict inflation or deflation.

Purchasing gold bars to store at home is impractical and expensive in most senses. Gold stored at home will lose value because its purity becomes suspect once it leaves a bank. You will have to pay for bars to be re-assayed before you can trade it in for money. In addition, there are limited amounts of gold you can store in your home, and the IRS will tax you on the value of the gold in the same way they tax other collectable item gains. You also will be charged 5% of the market price each time you buy or sell it.

If you feel you want to invest in precious metals, a small amount (about $150 - $250) can be purchased in the form of coins. Precious metal coins are easier to carry in the case of a survival situation. They are also easier to use for bartering than what gold bars or gold bank holdings would be.

Emergency cash

In addition to emergency money in a savings account, you should also keep about $120 in small bills and coins stored inside your house with your basic survival kit. This money is for disasters that may affect your ability to reach the bank.

Bartering basics

The key to being able to barter after a disaster is to have something that the other person wants. In a disaster situation, most people want their basic needs. If you can provide food, water, shelter, transportation, medical supplies, a method of communicating with others, gasoline, or transportation you have a better chance of achieving your wants. You may have your grandmother's antique doll collection that is worth a great deal of money, but most people left around after a disaster will find that not important.

If you want to barter successfully, stockpile extra items for each of your needs. Ensure that you have an effective means of communicating with the outside world. Learn valuable skills that people will need. Money and precious metal coinage can also be useful for bartering, but do not expect fair market value for your goods.

Part II: Preparing Your Basic Needs

Chapter 7: Water

How much water do you need to store in case of a disaster?

To protect yourself from dehydration and unsanitary conditions, you should store one gallon of water per person per day. Ideally, you will store thirty days worth of water, but you should have at least three days worth in your basic survival kit as a minimum amount.

If supplies are short, use stored water to drink and purified water to wash and clean.

How should I keep my stored water safe?

The best way to store water is in airtight FDA-approved DOT #34 containers. These are opaque, but water should still be stored in the dark. Do not store the containers in your garage or around paint, chemicals, pesticides, or gasoline. Make sure the water will not freeze while it is being stored. If you are storing water from a well or other untreated source, you should pre-treat it with 4 drops of chlorine bleach per gallon. Replace all the water every six months unless you have used a commercially available water preserver prior to storage.

Water should be stored in containers of differing sizes. If you are using the smaller containers for your day to day use, it will lower the chances the bigger containers have of becoming contaminated. You should also have containers that are clearly marked for both potable and non-potable water. Keep a portable three gallon container as a part of your basic survival kit.

Where can I find back up water resources?

If you run out of water supplies and you are at home, you can find more water in your hot water heater. You can also get water from the tanks of your toilet but not the bowls. Waterbeds and swimming pools may seem like ideal sources for water, but they contain contamination that cannot be removed. Do not use water from these sources to drink. Water from streams, lakes, or rivers can be used, but needs to be purified before you drink it. Installing rain barrels is another way to store water for emergencies. However, they need to be in place long before a disaster strikes to be useful during one.

If you are not at home and you are running low on water, you can collect dew from plants in the morning by soaking it up with a cloth, such as a bandana, and squeezing it into a collection container. You can also use twist ties to attach clear plastic bags around the leafy branches of trees. Water will collect in the sunlight. Solar stills are an excellent way to collect pure water, but they are difficult to build. If you are interested in using this technique for post-disaster water collection, it is recommended you practice by building one or two before a disaster strikes. You can work on perfecting your technique and save time and effort setting one up after a disaster.

Do not use seawater or brackish water as a water source unless you have a desalination device. Also, cloudy or murky water should be strained through a clean cloth before purifying it or filtering it.

How can I filter water?

Filtering murky, brackish or cloudy water can be as easy as pouring it through a funnel stuffed with a clean cloth or coffee filter. This will remove most of the bigger particles. However, this will not purify the water or make it safe to drink. It should only be used as a step before purification.

Some water filters sold commercially also double as water purifiers. Purchasing a portable water filter with an absolute pore size of less than one micron is an excellent idea and can be helpful in a pinch. Also, make sure to review the information about what the filter will remove. Be sure to purchase a supply of filters along with the filtering device.

What are different ways to purify water for drinking?

Although some may complain that it makes the water taste flat, boiling is the easiest way to purify water. Bringing water to a rolling boil for ten minutes has always been the standard for getting rid of disease causing microorganisms. It requires a pan and a source of heat.

Using iodine or chlorine are the second most popular ways to purify water. With cloudy water, you use sixteen drops of chlorine bleach (or ¼ teaspoon) or ½ teaspoon of iodine (about fifty drops) to purify a gallon of water. If the water is clear, you can use half that amount. Both forms of chemical purification have portable tablet forms that can be purchased from survival suppliers. Iodine is not recommended for pregnant women or people with thyroid problems. There are also people with iodine sensitivities. No matter what, iodine should not be used for more than a couple of weeks at a time.

Using chemicals or boiling water can both affect the taste. Ascorbic acid helps with off-flavors and can be purchased in pharmacies. For other ways of purifying water, you may try distilling or using a solar still.

How can I distill water?

Commercial distillers are available for purchase, but they are expensive. They can also require a lot of fuel if you use one that is not electric.

You can make a homemade distiller, but remember the distilling process is relatively slow. Because of the long period of time required, begin as soon as you realize you need to use this method of purifying water. Fill a large pot ½ of the way full with water. Float a tempered glass bowl on top of the water. Put a clean lid on the pot, upside down. Bring the water in the pot to a boil. As the water boils, it should drip into the bowl. Use hot pads to empty the bowl into coffee mugs to cool. (Note: if the water in the bowl begins to boil, you have the fire too hot.)

If I find myself running low on water, how can I conserve it in an emergency?

The first step to not running out of water is to have identified and capitalized on alternate water sources. Rain barrels or a solar still in place before a disaster can provide continued hydration during one. However, in any emergency situation water should be conserved as much as possible.

Conserving water does not mean limiting how much you drink. Everyone should be allowed a minimum of six, eight ounce cups of water per day to keep from dehydrating. It is better to drink what you need and keep your body functioning properly than to reduce the amount you consume to make it stretch longer. Dehydration is accumulative, and it reduces your ability to function.

You can recycle the water you are not drinking. For example, wash dishes, then use that water to wash clothes, and then use that water to flush the toilet. Use water you washed vegetables in to water the garden. Take sponge baths. Fill a gallon bowl with water and use a washcloth to wash your body from it. Once you a finished, use the non-potable water to flush the toilet. Assign everyone their own drinking cup, so you do not have to wash dishes over and over again. Go a step further and only use paper items for eating and drinking. To brush your teeth with minimal water, fill your drinking glass with water and dip your toothbrush in it. Add the toothpaste and finish brushing your teeth. Take a mouthful of water and swish, and then spit over your toothbrush to rinse it. If you feel it is necessary, you can repeat this process two more times, and then drink the rest of the water. Use water to cook vegetables or macaroni, and then reuse it to make soup or dried beans. Stop shaving – there is a reason why most television shows depict male survivalists with a beard.

Chapter 8: Food

How much food should I store for a disaster?

Enough food to last for a month is a feasible amount to store for a disaster. However, this does not mean that you should stock up on a hundred pounds of dried beans. You need to make sure the food you store is in proportion to nutrition guidelines and is varied enough to encourage you to eat it.

Based on nutritional guidelines, an average person needs twenty-four ounces of milk or three servings of a milk based product like pudding, six ounces of protein from meat or beans, four to six cups of fruits and vegetables, and four to six cups of grains each day. If you store a variety of foods that meet these needs, you will eat well even in the worst disaster situations.

How should I store my food?

You should store your food as close to forty degrees Fahrenheit as possible. The room you choose should be as dry as possible. Never place containers with food in them directly on the floor. Instead, you can place them on pallets or shelves. Like water, do not store food around hazardous chemicals, but do store it in containers that are opaque. Light can ruin food just as easily as it does water. Be sure to rotate your stock of stored food on a monthly basis.

As a general rule, you should also make sure all food is stored in airtight, food-grade, plastic or glass containers. Although these sealed containers will not help against the pests that have traveled home in the food, they will prevent pests from getting inside while you are storing it. If you want to ensure that there are no living pests in the food you are preparing to store, freeze the food, especially flours, for ten days.

What are the most important foods to stock pile?

It is necessary to have a variety of foods, but some foods are more suited for disaster survival. If you do not mind the cost, camping supply stores have a variety of dehydrated and freeze-dried meals you can choose from that are relatively easy to prepare and are palatable.

MREs (meals ready to eat) are what the military feeds soldiers in the field and sometimes the government ships them to disaster areas. They are not officially available to the public for purchase, but that does not stop people from selling them online. Because of this, MREs are riskier than dehydrated foods. The shelf life of a MRE is dependent on how they were stored. On average, they will last three years, but they can go rancid much quicker than that if they are stored at temperatures above eighty degrees. The other risk is that some people claim to be selling MREs but are not. There are many MRE styled off brands that may not have the quality or shelf-life of government issued MRE.

If you would prefer to make your own food from scratch, there are more options available. Some of the best foods to stock pile are canned and dried foods. Canned and jarred foods can provide a variety of fruits, vegetables, and soups. You can also have meats like salmon, tuna, chicken, and ham. Evaporated milk, lemon juice, and other juices can give variety to what you drink and preserve your water stores. Honey, pickles, olives, oils, peanut butter, jelly, and chilies will meet your dietary needs with variety. When looking for dried foods you can purchase dried fruits and vegetables, but you can also purchase baking mixes, such as those for pancakes, that just require for you to add water. Other suitable dried foods are staples for baking such as oatmeal, sugar, rice, powdered milk, salt, cocoa, flour, powdered eggs. Items to flavor you water like bullion, coffee, tea, and hot cocoa will help keep you hydrated and warm. Beans, pasta, dry cereal, instant potatoes, and dried eggs will help balance your diet. Some other foods you might want to consider are popcorn (not microwave), prepackaged pudding or Jell-O, energy bars, and candy. Choose only food that your family will eat. Nobody wants to suffer a substantial disaster only to find pickled pig's feet and borscht are the only options available for every meal.

Should I stockpile non-foods?

While food is often the first thing people want to secure in times of disaster, some non-food items are equally beneficial to stockpile before a disaster strikes. For example, toilet paper, paper towels, aluminum foil, plastic wrap, and garbage bags are all essential survival items.

It is also important to have a multivitamin on hand. When you are operating under stress and with a limited diet, you may not be getting vital nutrients. By taking a daily multivitamin, you will make sure your body stays healthy.

As a part of you non-food stockpile, include pots, pans, and an easy to use hand can opener (these are more expensive, but worth it if you will be opening cans by hand).

If you have an infant or child in diapers, be sure to stockpile all the items in the baby survival kit like diapers, moist towelettes, and diaper rash cream.

What are different ways to preserve food?

You can preserve your own food by standard methods of canning or pressure canning or by drying your foods. You may have to purchase special equipment to preserve foods in either of these ways. People who preserve their own food usually have a larger variety on hand for disaster situations. When you grow and then preserve your own food, you reduce you food costs drastically.

Without special equipment, you can try using cold storage or a root cellar to store fruits and vegetables. You do not have to dig a root cellar, but you can use a cold closet or a cold corner of a basement. Some fruits and vegetables prefer moisture, others do not. The ideal cold storage place will be completely dark, have an even, cool temperature, and be sealed well from pests. You will need to keep some fruits and vegetables away from each other if you are using this method of preservation (apples and potatoes do not keep well together). Also, some vegetables may need special treatment before storing (carrots should be stored layered in sand).

How do I can food?

Canning can be a fun and satisfying activity, but it takes a considerable amount of time to do. You must prepare the jars in a hot water canner or pressure canner, prepare your recipe (only use recipes that have been tested by a reliable source), load your jars and release extra air, clean your rims, seal, process in the canner, allow to sit, and finally clean the jars and test to see if they have sealed. When you can, you must purchase the canner, special jars, rims, lids, canning tongs, strainers, nonmetal spatulas, and a wide-mouthed funnel.

Pressure canning is the only way to can foods with low acidity, such as meats and non-pickled vegetables. It is particularly important to purchase a new, modern pressure canner to prevent horrible accidents. While most canning supplies can be reused, it is necessary to replace the lids every year. Old lids may not seal and then you will need to eat the food within twenty-four hours to save it.

There are canning books on the market by Ball and the USDA that should be purchased and studied if you are interested in canning. You should also start by helping someone else do it. It is a fast paced job and you are frequently making the next item while sealing a prior one. You should plan on spending one to two days canning each item in bulk. It is helpful if you have a dishwasher to heat the jars.

How do I dehydrate or freeze dry food?

Unlike canning, dehydrating or drying foods requires little special equipment. There are dehydrators, but you can also dry foods in your oven (you might have to purchase an oven thermometer to ensure the temperature remains between 120 and 140 degrees Fahrenheit). Some people even dry food in the sun.

The other benefits of dehydrating food are that it is easier to learn than canning, and you can make your own recipes. On the down side foods, especially vegetables, do not retain the same texture, look, or taste when they are dried. Also, foods that are not dried properly can get moldy. Finally, some foods need to be stored in plastic bags that do not allow light to penetrate them.

How do I start and plan a garden?

The first thing needed for starting a garden is a place to put it. You do not need to have a large plot of land to start a garden. In fact, you can make a nice one with hanging planters on any porch. After you find a place to have your garden, you should consult the library for books on gardening so you can improve your gardening skills. Like any skill, gardening takes time and patience. Accept that one year, a plant might grow well and the next year it might do poorly.

If your garden is in the ground, you will need to put a tight fence around it to keep animals from eating it. Chicken wire that is two feet wide and metal posts should work well enough. Also, some plants will need something to grow on like a trellis or cage. You can purchase these or make them yourself.

For a hanging garden, good plants to choose are tomatoes, cucumbers, beans, lettuce, and strawberries. For a traditional in ground garden, choose tomatoes, beans, potatoes, peas, peppers, and lettuce.

Which animals would be good to raise in an emergency?

If you live in the city, your options are limited as to what you can raise. However, if you have a backyard, chickens are good options for people looking to survive a disaster with fresh food. Chickens provide not only meat but also eggs. They are small enough to be kept with a moderate yard in a suburb and can easily be brought inside in temporary emergencies. You can purchase a large dog cage to confine them.

If you live in the country and have even more space, I recommend purchasing goats. Goats provide milk that is similar in taste to whole milk. If your family does not like it as a drink, you can at least use it in recipes. They are relatively easy to care for, and they also can be slaughtered if your family is in need of meat or bartering material.

Chapter 9: Shelter During a Disaster

How can I prevent my home from being destroyed by a disaster?

Because some disasters come without warning, it is an excellent idea to prepare your home in advance for them. You can do some things for your home to prepare.

Inside your home, make sure that all beds are arranged away from windows. Windows are a vulnerable place in any home. You do not want to sleep next to them. Store heavy items low, so that they will not fall on anyone during a disaster. Be sure that pictures, shelves, and wall ornaments are well secured to the wall. Every home should also have working smoke detectors on each level. Make sure all hallways are clear and easy to navigate in case you need to evacuate your home in a hurry. If you have bedrooms on upper levels, consider investing in a ladder. A small fire extinguisher should be kept in the kitchen and tested regularly. Be sure to store all flammable and reactive chemicals in a well-ventilated area that children cannot access.

You should perform seasonal inspections outside your home to ensure it is ready to keep you safe during a disaster. Make sure shingles are secure. Trim trees that are near your home. Consider removing trees and branches that could fall on your roof or break windows during a disaster.

Check overhangs and carports to ensure that they are well-supported. These could collapse during disasters. Check to see if your overhead garage door has a securing bolt on the inside. If this is missing, drill a hole in the track and create one with a lock. Make sure the door from the house into your garage and all other outside doors are solid core steel and consider creating a safe room.

Do I need special products to prepare my home to prepare for a disaster?

Certain items are beneficial to help keep your home secure during a disaster. Smoke and carbon monoxide detectors, as well as radon detectors (in areas at risk), can save you and your family by providing an early warning. Fire extinguishers can stop fires before they become unmanageable.

A tool kit with hand tools that work when the electricity does not is vital. Supplies to repair your home, such as extra shingles, plywood, plastic sheeting, tarps, and 2 x 4's will help keep you home secure if it sustains damage during a disaster. Your home repair tool kit should include:

- Hammers
- Nails
- Screws
- Screw drivers (Phillips or cross and flat)
- Adjustable wrenches
- Tapes – duct, electrical, transparent
- Hand saw
- Super glue and wood glue
- Shovel
- Ax
- Utility knife
- Clamps
- Pliers
- Crow bars
- Basic home repair manual

Firearms and ammunition are beneficial as long as you are prepared to use them. Generators can keep the power running even when the power grid has stopped working. Green houses can allow you to produce fresh food year long. A wood pile and wood stove can keep you warm when the furnace is not working.

Now that I am ready, should I purchase a firearm to protect my home from looters?

Whether or not to purchase a firearm depends on whether you will use it to defend your home. If you only want it to *threaten* looters and are not planning on shooting anyone, it will be in your best interest to learn more passive ways of defending your home. Regardless of your choice on weapons, all members of your family should learn some form of self-defense.

To defend your home passively, enroll in a self-defense class. Install bars on your windows that will allow you to escape in case of fire or other emergency but will deter other people from getting inside. Get a watchdog (a good option for anyone). A watchdog does not have to be mean; it just has to be big and barks loud. Even nice, large dogs will defend their families. (A small one might try to defend its family too but will not intimidate looters. To make matters worse, a little dog may be hurt or killed in the process of defending you.)

To defend your home actively, your best option is using firearms. You can invest in all the passive methods, but having a weapon that causes immediate damage is a strong benefit for those who are able to use it. With any weapon, it is important to have training in how to use it safely. It is also important to practice using it. If you have children, they should be educated in the use of all weapons in the home, but should not be allowed to access any of them without supervision. They should also be required to take firearm safety courses. There are many lockable cases to prevent unsupervised access. Be sure to use them. If there is a disaster situation that requires you to use your weapon, you will have enough advanced warning to retrieve it from a locked case. If you do not secure your firearms, you may create your own disaster when a family member dies because the weapon was handled improperly.

The easiest firearm to use is a shotgun. You do not have to aim well because the shot scatters in a wide spray. The down side is you only have about six shots before you must reload. In addition, while the large size of the weapon makes it useful without ammunition, it also makes it easier to take the weapon away from you. Other firearms, such as rifles and handguns, require better accuracy, but offer more shots before you need to reload. Some people find it difficult to hunt with a handgun. Keep this in mind if you are purchasing a weapon. It is always good to have another method of obtaining food. Bows and crossbows only have one shot. If you already have them and know how to use them, fine, but these are not weapons recommended for the beginner trying to defend his or her home. Finally, there are other weapons, such as tasers, knives, swords, and martial arts weapons. If you know how to use them, and they are already a part of your home, they can be helpful. However, these should not be purchased with only the goal of defending your home during a disaster in mind.

How do I keep my important documents safe?

Safe deposit boxes are good, offsite storage places for important documents. However, a safe deposit box may become inaccessible during a disaster. Another option is to keep important papers in a fireproof safe inside your home. Some papers that you may need during a disaster are:

To keep on your person:

- Driver's licenses
- Credit cards and insurance cards
- Weapon's permits
- Medical information
- Emergency contact information

To keep in a central place in your home:

- Disaster plan
- First aid information booklet
- Survival references
- Maps and directions to all meeting points

To keep in your home safe:

- Insurance policies and home inventory with video/photos
- Recent pay stub and resume

- Professional licenses
- Bank account, Credit card account, and investment information
- Tax records
- Computer accounts, logins, and passwords
- Passports and Social Security cards
- Recent high-quality photos of family members
- Description of all vehicles
- Marriage license
- Firearm serial numbers, makes, and models
- Birth certificates/death certificates/adoption papers
- Immunization records

To keep in a safe deposit box:

- Will and advance directives
- Property deeds and vehicle titles
- DD214 or other military papers
- Diplomas/certificates
- Contracts, promissory notes, deeds
- Certificates for stocks and bonds

How can I secure my home once a disaster has occurred?

If you are told you need to evacuate your home immediately, do not take time to secure it. Just get out with your basic survival kit. Your vehicle survival kits should always be in the vehicle you would use if you needed to evacuate.

If you have time to plan before you leave your home behind, you will want it to be secure. If appropriate, shut down power, heating, and water systems (including your water heater), and if appropriate, unplug all appliances. Secure all windows and doors by bracing them if necessary. Take your most valuable items with you and your survival packs plus as much water and food as you can. Make a list of important things you would like to take and try to have one or two other people look at it to see if there is something you are forgetting.

Chapter 10: Your Safe Room

What is a safe room?

A safe room is a room inside your home that is structurally sound and capable of protecting you from disasters that may occur in your area (for example, a safe room for a flood would be located on top floors, whereas a safe room for a tornado should be in a basement). If you can remain in your home during a disaster, these provide an added net of safety.

How can I build a safe room?

You can create a safe room from any interior room in your house. It is best to have a minimum of ten square feet of space per person using the room. Exchange the door leading to your safe room for a secure one.

Some companies offer solid, safe room kits for between $5,000 and $15,000. Investing in a quality kit may be a good idea if you have no other way to create a safe room in your home. Look into all the costs (will you be able to set it up by yourself or will you have to hire someone) and compare several styles and companies in order to find one that suits your family's needs. Cheapest is not always the best. Any quality safe room kit will contain a way to filter air.

What should be stored in a safe room?

Primarily, you should stock the safe room with your disaster kits. The supplies you have stockpiled should be stored close to it, but you only need about two weeks worth of food and water inside it. You need a light source and a radio that do not require electricity in order to run. A whistle is also important to signal rescue workers if needed. A non-electric can opener, toiletries, and a bucket or two for waste disposal are also good to keep inside the safe room initially.

Other things you should remember to provide are pillows, blankets, and items for entertainment and comfort. Plastic sheeting and duct tape are also useful supplies for your safe room. You should also keep an ax, hand saw (in case you need to cut your way out), and a flare gun in it. If using battery operated items have enough batteries for two weeks. If you have any firearms, it is an excellent idea to store them securely in here as well.

Chapter 11: Hygiene and Sanitation during an Emergency or Disaster

How can I stay clean during a disaster?

Cleanliness during a disaster is important. Disease is easier to contract when you are going through high stress events. Combine that with the naturally lower sanitation levels as sewage and other contaminants are release from broken pipes and flooded sewers, and you have a recipe for making a bad disaster worse. Just because the power has gone out and the water no longer works does not mean you need to live in squalor.

Each person needs to drink between forty-eight and sixty-four ounces of water per day. If you have stored a gallon of water for each person per day, that leaves about a half gallon for hygienic purposes. You will be able to brush your teeth, wash hands, and maybe even have a sponge bath, but not much more than that. All potable water should be recycled as much as possible. Use disposable utensils and dishes. Wash only socks and underwear.

Using antibacterial sanitizer and wipes will prove a good way to say clean when you cannot use water. Rubbing alcohol will clean most non-food surfaces. Witch hazel is an excellent astringent and can be used to clean the face. Finding a non-potable supply of water is also helpful for flushing toilets.

What is a sanitary hygiene kit?

When preparing for a disaster, food often gets high priority, while sanitation is not even thought about. The problem is that poor sanitation leads to sickness. In disaster situations, medicine for even the simplest diseases may not be attainable. To prepare for your sanitation needs during a disaster and to prevent sickness consider creating a sanitary hygiene kit:

- Chlorine bleach (three bottles)

- Vinegar (one gallon)
- Heavy duty plastic garbage bags (sixty to one hundred)
- Several rolls of toilet paper (enough to last two months)
- Antibacterial moist towelettes (ten packs)
- Liquid dish detergent (can double for hand washing laundry)
- Toothpaste (two tubes) and baking soda (four boxes)
- Hydrogen peroxide (six bottles) and rubbing alcohol (three bottles)
- Feminine needs (enough for two months)
- Antibacterial hand sanitizer (one bottle per person)
- Several stacks of washcloths to be used for towels or wipes (thirty to sixty)
- Disposable dishes and utensils (enough for ninety meals per person)
- Camp stove and fuel (enough for thirty days)
- Waterless shampoo
- Four five-gallon buckets with tight lids
- Toilet seat (one or two)
- Two weeks' worth of clean socks and undergarments per person
- N95 to N100 face masks – NIOSH approved (thirty or reusable ones)
- Diapers and wet wipes are also important if you have a baby

Removing waste in the home.

If you have a source of non-potable water and the sewer lines are not broken, it is recommended that you continue using your toilets. Dumping an excess of water into the toilet causes it to flush. Once you flush the toilet in this way, make sure some water remains in the bottom of the bowl to prevent harmful sewer gases from escaping into your home. Flush only when a person has a bowel movement and before going to bed at night to conserve water. If the sewer lines are broken, you can line the toilet bowl with a heavy duty trash bag and remove after someone has a bowel movement.

Prior to a disaster, you can install a composting toilet that does not use electricity. These are very expensive and require daily maintenance, but will work like normal during a disaster.

Garbage can be thrown into a composting toilet, compost pile, or buried deeply in the backyard (especially in a garden plot). Trash needs to be bagged and stored unless it is a paper product. Paper products can be used as tinder to light fires or can be hand shredded and treated as compost.

Portable waste management.

The most portable way to manage waste is by using five-gallon buckets. These buckets can store solid waste, liquid waste, garbage, and trash. When their lids are sealed, they can prevent bad odors from permeating your abode. They also can be carried in the car.

If you are on the go and have a shovel, you can dig your own toilet or latrine pretty much anywhere. Make sure you are not within fifty feet of any water source or well. Dig down about two to three feet (deeper if there are more people in your group) and let everyone use it. Then cover it again before leaving (unless you are using this method as a stationary waste management system).

Preventing the spread of disease.

Hand washing is the best way to prevent the spread of disease. If someone in your family gets sick during a disaster, limit that person's exposure to the other people. Wearing a N95, N99, or N100 face mask is important when dealing with a sickness caused by a biological weapon or pandemic. Every time another family member has contact with the sick person, they should wash or sanitize their hands.

If a person gets a wound that breaks the skin – a cut, scrape, or even a bug bite – make sure to disinfect the area as soon as possible. Cover it with a clean bandage, but allow it to air at night.

Everything that deals with waste should be kept outside your home. If you still have toilets that you can manually flush, you can use non-potable water to flush them and remove waste. If your toilets do not work, you will need to use buckets or toilet bowls lined with heavy duty trash bags to go to the bathroom. Store buckets outside or in the garage, one for solid and one for liquid waste. Each day, you will need to dig a deep hole and bury the bag of solid waste. The bag of liquid waste can be dumped in a shallow trench about a foot deep and then cover with a layer of dirt. If you cannot bury your waste, add contractor bags to your sanitation kit and store the bagged waste in there.

Food scraps should be scraped into a composting pile or fed to pets. If you do not have either of these options, bury them outside. Do not attempt to save food from one meal to the next.

Part III: Preparing for Secondary Needs

Chapter 12: Medical needs

Learning basic first aid

Never walk into a dangerous situation to try to help someone else. For example, if it is rainy, electric wires are down, and you see a person lying in a puddle of water, do not try to pull them out. The electricity could flow into your body as well. If a structure is unstable, and you rush into it in order to save someone, you could suffer severe harm.

Be careful in learning first aid from books and the internet. There are several books and websites on first aid that contain misinformation when it comes to lifesaving techniques. Some techniques have the potential of cracking ribs even if done correctly so use with care. If you perform CPR on a person who does not need it, you can kill him or her. Even the simplest procedures can go wrong if you do not know what you are doing, or you learned poor skills from an unreliable source. For example, you may know how to place a piece of clean fabric on a wound and apply pressure to stop bleeding. However, say you then check in a few minutes to see if it is still bleeding. If you remove the cloth, you can cause the bleeding to start again even if it had stopped.

Children as young as twelve can take a basic first aid course at the local Red Cross. It is highly recommended that you and the other members of your family get certified in community first aid and CPR. If you are willing to stock your home for a disaster, you should also be willing to learn how to save those around you during medical emergencies. Get proper training from the Red Cross and be assured that you will know the most up-to-date techniques for saving your loved ones.

Making homemade disinfectant

The easiest homemade disinfectant is bleach water. Made with one cup of bleach and nine cups of water, it is a strong disinfectant. It will destroy most pathogens and also helps mask bad smells. Surfaces that you plan on using to prepare food should be rinsed after using bleach water. Also, it will use some of your water stores to make this disinfectant.

If you are looking for a less harsh alternative, spray hydrogen peroxide first and then spray vinegar on the surface to be disinfected. You do not need to rinse the surface in order to prepare food on it. However, the hydrogen peroxide needs to be stored in a dark bottle because it breaks down in the presence of light. Also, do not mix the hydrogen peroxide and vinegar in advance or they will be useless.

Stocking a disaster first aid kit

You may think buying a first aid kit at the store is the first thing anyone should do if they want to prepare for an emergency. Keep in mind that these kits often contain a bare minimum of items at a high cost (although the packaging is usually reusable and nice). To make your own first aid kit from scratch, purchase a portable bag and stock it with:

- Hydrogen peroxide, rubbing alcohol, iodine, and cotton balls
- Sun block, lip balm, and bug spray
- Triple antibiotic ointment
- 5% Cortisone cream
- Tweezers, needles, safety pins, and a magnifying glass
- Calcium and salicylic based stomach medicine
- Loratadine and diphenhydramine based antihistamines
- Ibuprofen and acetaminophen
- Benzocaine toothache relief
- Antidiarrheal medicine. laxatives, and antipurgatives
- Pseudoephedrine and guaifenesin cold remedies
- Thermometer

- Variety of adhesive bandages and butterfly closures (at least two hundred)
- Gauze pads and first aid tape
- Four cloth slings and wood to make a splint
- Elastic bandage
- Hot and cold packs
- Disposable gloves
- Tongue depressors
- Powdered electrolyte replacement
- Small flashlight
- Budget sanitary napkins
- Small scissors and larger ones to cut away contaminated clothing
- First aid manual

Be sure to learn how to use each item in your kit before you need to use it.

Making an electrolyte solution to keep you hydrated

You do not have to purchase a pre-made electrolyte replacement solution. You can make your own from scratch if your stock is depleted. Here is a quick and easy recipe:

Dissolve 2 teaspoons honey in 4 cups hot water. Add ¼ teaspoon salt and ¼ cup lemon juice. Allow to cool.

Which over-the-counter medications should I have on hand?

You should have a thirty day supply of all the medicines recommended in the first aid kit. Medicines lose their effectiveness over time. Check expiration dates monthly and replace what has expired. An ineffective medicine is useless for disaster survival.

Also, make sure you have a form of the medicine that is appropriate for each age group in your family. A toddler will need a chewable or liquid form, while adults need more concentrated pills to swallow.

Stockpiling prescription medications

Prescription medicines are more vital to have on hand than over the counter drugs, but are also very difficult to stockpile. Consider checking with your doctor to see if you are eligible to purchase three month supplies of your medicines. This is the easiest and safest way to have enough medicine on hand for any disaster. Some doctors may also allow you to have a disaster prescription. Just remember that prescription medicine will lose effectiveness after one year like any other medication. Whenever you renew your prescription, switch out the disaster stock with the new stock and take the old pills first.

Chapter 13: Communicating

What is an out-of-state contact?

Sometimes disasters, like an earthquake, affect a large area. More than one household in your family may be affected. In these situations, it is an excellent idea to have an out-of-state contact. This is a person, usually a relative, who everyone in the family knows to call when things go wrong. Instead of having fifty people trying to get in contact with each other, the main contact gets the information and relays it as others check in. If parents and children who know an out-of-state contact are separated, they can check-in and find each other again.

How to stay connected during a disaster.

When securing yourself for a disaster, it is important to remain connected to the rest of the world. Normally, we connect through phones, radio, television, and the internet. When disasters occur, frequently lines of communication are cut. Phone circuits become bogged down, power fails, and we can become a lonely island.

Having a method of communicating during a disaster is important. Between family members, it may pay to purchase a simple low output walkie talkie or CB set that will allow one member of the family to go on short excursions while remaining connected to the rest of the family back home. Cell phones are also beneficial if they have texting capabilities, because when regular calls are blocking the networks, text messages can often make it through. If you plan on using your cell phone to communicate during an emergency, purchase a hand-crank flashlight that doubles as a cell phone charger.

HAM Radios

Another method of relaying information is a HAM radio. These are radio stations run by average people broadcast on the AM network.

When other means of communication have failed, these still operate because they come from a person's home. If you are interested in becoming a HAM radio operator, do a quick internet search and find a group of operators to join that appeals to you. They will help you get started.

Keeping on top of the news

The most effective way to keep track of the news during a disaster is through a radio. Hand crank radios do not require batteries, but some are put together poorly and break easily. The benefit is you may be able to power other items, such as your cell phone, with it.

Battery powered televisions are another choice for those wanting to keep track of how the outside world is faring, but if the disaster is too widespread, there may not be any television transmissions.

Chapter 14: Electrical Power

What do I do in a power outage?

The first thing to do in a power outage is to find out what caused the outage and about how long it is estimated the outage will continue. You can listen to a battery operated or hand crank radio to find out the information you need to know.

The next thing you should do is provide alternate lighting. If you notice the sun is still in the sky, all the better. It will make finding your alternate light sources easier.

Finally, you need to unplug anything electrical so that you can protect it from a power surge when the electricity comes back. Tape the refrigerator and freezer doors closed to help remind people not to open them. This will prolong the life of your perishable food.

If you have a generator, schedule times when you will use it (early morning before the sun is up and right after the sun goes down are the best times). There are a variety of generators from gas powered to human powered on the market. Select one that will work the best for your family.

Power failure kit

During a power failure, it is important to have all the supplies you need together in one place, since you will probably need to find them with little or no light. Although you cannot keep lanterns that run on fuels or the fuels themselves in a tote, the nonflammable items should be stored together in a container with glow-in-the-dark tape on the outside. It is better to use items with batteries than items with fuel or flames. Items with fuel or flames can make the disaster worse by catching your house on fire. Some items you may need when the power goes out are:

- Telephone that plugs into the wall (not cordless)

- Candles (be careful)
- Lantern (propane or kerosene with extra wicks and fuel)
- Battery operated or hand crank flashlights and lanterns
- Glow sticks (for children)
- Matches or lighter
- Cook stove and fuel

Generators are good backups during a power outage. All generators (except human powered ones) should be operated outside. Find out how much energy your furnace, washing machine, and one or two other essentials use and purchase a generator that will meet your needs. You will need to have the generator professionally installed so you can switch off the grid and onto the generator during power outages. You will also have to store fuel for the generator. Human powered generators are a poor option because they require a lot of effort for a little amount of energy generated. They will not be able to run major appliances.

How do I start a camp fire?

You should always practice lighting a fire before you need to do it. Practice in wet weather, dry weather, and at night. If you have a fireplace or wood burning stove, you need to make sure the damper is open before starting a fire in it.

To start a campfire outside, you need to form a fire ring. You can use an old metal tire rim, or you can use a shovel to clear the grass away from a three foot circle. Line the edge of the circle with large rocks or bricks. There are three different wood formations that work well to build a fire: the A-frame, the cabin, and the bonfire.

For the A-frame, which is the easiest, make a pile of tinder the size of one hand wrapped around your other fist. Tinder is dry pine needles, paper, and small twigs (no bigger than the width of three pine needles). Pinecones can also be used, but they can be difficult to light initially. Around your pile of tinder make an "A" or triangle out of twigs no bigger than a pencil in width. When your walls of small twigs get to be about two-inches tall, begin using thumb sized twigs. When these make the structure a total of four inches tall, add sticks that are about one-inch in diameter (until each of the three sides has two one-inch sticks). Carefully poke a match through a gap in one of the walls toward the base and light the tinder. When the one-inch sticks catch on fire, add four-inch logs using the same "A" pattern. As soon as the four-inch logs catch on fire, you can add a smaller split log and do not have to follow the pattern, as long as you do not crush the fire (in other words, do not throw it directly on top of the fire, but position it so it is only covering one side).

To light a fire, you can use matches, but sometimes it is better to use butane lighter to light a piece of tinder and then use the tinder to light the rest of the fire. Butane lighters will throw sparks that you can start a fire with even when they are out of fuel. There are other ways to start fires without matches, such as flint and steel kits or by rubbing two pieces of wood together, but these can be tricky and require much more practice. The easiest way to light a fire without a match or lighter is to build your tinder pile over a stretched out piece of steel wool. The steel wool should have contact points on both sides of the tinder. Attach a pair of jumper cables to a car battery that has been disconnected and then touch them to either side of the steel wool as if you are jump starting it. The steel wool should catch on fire, and that should ignite the tinder.

In damp or wet weather, you should be able to light dry wood and tinder just as easily as you did in dry weather. However, if you tinder or your wood is wet, plan on using a large amount of matches and dry paper to get your fire started. Once you start a fire in wet weather, always keep a round of logs just inside your fire ring but not in your fire (never leave them unattended). This will help dry them out. In wet weather, it is especially important to keep your fire going all day long, but bank it at night. To bank a fire, scatter the embers until the flames are gone and cover with a light layer of dirt. To restart a banked fire, uncover the embers and bring them back together. Build you next fire on top of the embers. If you have practiced this, you may be able to get it to restart without a match.

How do I cook without electricity?

Unless you have a fireplace or wood stove and you have practiced cooking on them, you will need to do all cooking outside. Cooking over an open fire is slightly easier than cooking on a woodstove because you can move the pot to alternate temperatures on an open flame. For the stove, you have to adjust the fuel. You can use a camp stove (be sure you have one of these and its fuel as a part of your basic survival supplies) or an outdoor grill. You can also make your own grill by lining a Dutch oven with foil, lighting charcoal in it, and putting a grate over the top. Keep a supply of fuel or charcoal and lighter fluid on hand. If you decide to cook from an open fire, you can build a wall of bricks on two sides of where the fire will be and stretch a grate across them. It is difficult to regulate temperatures over open flames, so it is best if you begin by cooking stews and soups. As you get more practice, you can find many camp cookbooks that will help improve your skills.

To bake during a power outage, you can use a solar oven. You can buy nice ones that get up to 375 degrees Fahrenheit on a cold day, but they are expensive. You also can make a small one out of a pizza box lined with aluminum foil. Cut three sides of a square in the lid and prop it open (the side that was inside the box should be covered with foil). Put the food you want to bake inside and seal the hole with plastic wrap. This solar oven will only get to about 200 degrees Fahrenheit on a nice day. You will need to cook fewer items for about twice as long as you normally would. Also, be sure your oven remains in direct sunlight throughout the day.

If you are ambitious, there are places that sell old-fashioned wood-burning or coal-burning cook stoves. If you install one of these and learn to use it, you will never have to worry about cooking outside during a power outage. Wood can burn in a coal burning stove, but never put coal in a wood stove. You can also still use gas stoves as long as there has not been a disaster such as an earthquake that could have destroyed the lines or one that required you to shut off the gas.

Heating and cooling the home during a power outage

A generator is the easiest way to heat and cool your home during a power outage. You will only be able to run the generator for short, scheduled, periods of time or you will run out of fuel. To make the most of it, get an energy audit done on your home by the power company and follow their instructions for keeping the temperature inside your home steady.

Without a generator, you can heat your home with a woodstove or a barrel stove. You can replace your furnace with a pellet stove, coal stove, or wood burning stove, but if you do this expensive switch, make sure the stove does not have an electric lighting mechanism. Other unique appliances are propane powered refrigerator/freezers and washing machines.

If the temperature remains below 40 degrees Fahrenheit, you can store items from your refrigerator outside in a cooler with a weight on top or in the garage near the garage door. If it stays below 32 degrees Fahrenheit, you can store freezer (and refrigerator) items in either of these places.

Chapter 15: Caring for Pets During a Disaster

How to prepare your pets for an emergency.

All pets have special needs to prepare for in case of an emergency. You pets should have collars and tags, or if they are confined to cages, they should have emergency contact information and care attached to their cages. All pets should be up to date on any shots and vaccinations and you should keep records of these in your home safe. Keep a colored, high definition photo of your pet so you can use it to make posters if the pet is lost. Also, all pets should have a kennel or cage to make transporting and containing them during a disaster easier.

Preparing pets to deal with a disaster requires training, especially for dogs. Teach your dog how to walk on a leash and with a harness. Also, practice indoor recreation with your dog, so it is prepared to exercise inside if you are confined to the house during a disaster. Even if your pet is gentle, they may become aggressive during a disaster. Purchasing a muzzle and getting your pet used to wearing it will not only reduce stress later, but make other people you come in contact with feel more comfortable.

A pet emergency kit

Pets have different needs from humans. Making a special evacuation kit for your pet and keeping it in a backpack that your pet can wear is an excellent idea. Here are things to pack it with:

- Pet food (the emergency kit should hold three days, but a thirty day stock is good)
- Non-spill bowls for food and water
- Potable water for your pet (a half gallon per day should be sufficient)
- Any pet medications (three day supply in kit; one month supply in kit)

- Sturdy leashes and or harnesses, muzzles, and portable cages
- Can opener and plastic can lid if your pet uses canned food
- Plastic bags, newspaper, litter, scoop, and litter box
- Rope and stake to tie animals while traveling

Keep in mind that pet supplies need to be rotated just as frequently as human supplies. Pet foods are also just as susceptible to pests so be sure to keep them in proper containers. Garbage cans with locking lids are a good way to store mass quantities of dry pet food. Do not change pet food during a disaster. If you feel it would be easier to work with canned food because they provide water, switch now. Conversely, if you feel it would be easier to store dry food, switch now.

What to do if a disaster occurs when you are separated from your pet.

Sometimes you may be away from your home when disaster strikes. It is always a good idea to have a friend or trusted neighbor, who is familiar to your pet, check on your animal for you. Ensure that this person has a spare key to your home.

Leaving a pet behind

If you are called upon to evacuate, you may not be able to take your pet with you. Temporary shelters that are established during emergencies will only allow service dogs with shot records and a physician statement that you need the animal for a medical reason. Many hotels also do not accept pets.

Pets left behind in your home should never be chained or tied. They should be confined to a limited space. Leave pets plenty of food and water; keep toilet lids up and bathroom doors open, so pets can have access to additional water. Leave a notice for rescue workers about where your animal is, what its name is, when you left the pet, and what type of pet you have. All areas are supposed to have plans in place for evacuating animals. Try not to leave your pet alone for more than two days. Also, try to have someone check on your pet while you are gone.

As an alternative, you may be able to find a veterinarian or animal boarding shelter that can take your pet.

Part IV: Exodus

Chapter 16: Transportation Before, During, and After a Disaster

Preparing your vehicle for a disaster.

A vehicle with no gas in it is not very helpful during a disaster. Try to always keep your vehicles half full of gas. If you hear a call to evacuate, you will be able to save time if you can at least get away from the general area before having to fill up your gas tank. Similarly, keeping your vehicle in good repair is another way of being prepared for any disaster. Also it is an excellent idea to keep a separate emergency kit and first aid kit in your vehicle.

Vehicle disaster kit

Vehicles come with their own special set of needs. It is always a good idea to learn how to take care of a few minor mechanical problems, such as filling up your windshield washer fluid, in case there is an emergency where you have to do it quickly. You can even practice changing a tire, just remember when you put the lug nut back on to tighten them in a star pattern, and make sure they are very tight. Things you should keep in your vehicle at all times include:

For repairs:

- Inflated spare tire in good repair, jack, lug nut wrench
- Tire repair kit
- Jumper cables (Black goes on negative first, Red goes on positive second – remember smoke before fire)
- Roofing shingles (for weight and traction) and collapsible shovel
- Extra fuses
- Duct tape

- Road flares
- Snow brush and scraper
- Premixed engine coolant (Never take the cap off the radiator when the engine is hot!)
- A quart of oil, power steering fluid (Get what your user manual recommends.)
- A quart of brake fluid (This should never be low unless you have a serious problem.)
- A gallon of windshield washer fluid
- Empty container approved to carry gasoline
- Screw drivers (Phillips and flat head)
- Two adjustable wrenches

Semi-trucks are required to carry fire extinguishers and some people think this is an excellent idea as well. However, during an accident the extinguisher can explode and ruin everything around it. If you are stranded, you will need additional supplies to survive. Always stay with the car if you are stranded.

In case you are stranded:

- A case of bottled water for every six people
- Non electric radio
- Flashlight
- Whistle
- Blankets (one per person, but large enough for two to share)
- Emergency cell phone
- Heavy duty trash bags (can double as rain ponchos)
- Spare diapers, wipes, baby food, and formula if you have an infant
- Six energy bars per person
- Butane lighter, collapsible stove, and fuel canister
- Sunscreen and insect repellant
- Multipurpose knife with saw function
- Three rolls of toilet paper and a box of tissue

Types of vehicles to use during recovery from a disaster

Transportation during disaster recovery may need to be very different than regular transportation. During disaster recovery, resources like fuel may be inaccessible. It is an excellent idea to have a motorized scooter or bicycle available to you. This will allow you to travel where you need to go without using resources you may need to conserve for evacuation, should the area become unstable.

Vehicles to use to evacuate after a disaster

Once a disaster occurs, navigating roads and escape routes becomes more difficult. Often the only ways to get into or out of disaster areas are blocked with traffic. If you underestimate a disaster and decide afterward that you need to evacuate, make sure you have the right vehicle to use for your escape.

The best vehicle will have 4 x 4 ability in case the road conditions are not clear. It will be in prime repair and will have the ability to carry your family and enough gear to survive for several days. Keep in mind that a vehicle that gets good gas mileage will take you further from the disaster area before making it necessary to stop and get gas. Remember to shut your engine and electronics off if you are stopped in traffic jams. Listen to the battery operated radio in your vehicle emergency kit instead.

Chapter 17: To Leave or Stay?

What is bugging out?

Bugging out is planning on leaving your area and finding a more permanent shelter. The total time it should take for you to transfer from one place to the next should be less than 72-hours, so your bug-out bag or basic survival kit contains supplies for that length of time.

A basic survival kit (bug out bag) is only the bare minimum an average person will need to survive for 3 days. If you plan to walk 15 miles per day (this is a light walk for average individuals), it will get you 45 miles away from the disaster.

If you can take more because you are able to use your vehicle, follow the guide for packing your vehicle and do so. People with special needs and children will also need additional supplies in their bug-out bag (see relative sections). You should practice carrying your bug-out bag around for an hour or so. If you find it is too heavy, consider purchasing a backpack with an internal or external frame to put your items inside. You should practice carrying it on park trails a few times a month to build up your endurance. A person who is trained in wilderness survival and backpacking may need less in their bag.

If you bug out, be sure to leave a note in a prominent place at your home that tells when you left and where you went. Also, be sure to lock your doors.

When should you consider evacuating?

Regardless of how prepared your house is for any disaster, if officials call for a mandatory evacuation, you should be the first to have you and your family on the road. Evacuations are never called lightly. If they are mandatory, remaining behind will not only put you and your family at risk, but also you will be putting the lives of the rescue workers on the line that come to save you.

Another reason you may want to evacuate is that you realize the severity of an impending situation, and you do not want to put your family at risk. Houses are demolished in a variety of disasters. No amount of stockpiled items can keep your home from being a victim. If you have advance warning and you believe the disaster will be bad, there is no reason to stay. Secure your house, pack your car, and evacuate.

The third reason you may decide to evacuate is after the disaster is finished. You may not have been given adequate warning. Or perhaps a mild hurricane turned into a major flood. You may be growing tired of eating canned food and living without flushable toilets. Whatever the reason, it is good that you recognize your limits and are ready to find a more secure location until the recovery is complete.

When should I use a temporary shelter

If your house has been compromised structurally, and it becomes unsafe to stay under your roof, you may want to consider building a temporary outdoor structure or putting up a tent. For example, during an earthquake, your home may have survived the initial movement, but aftershocks could cause it to tumble, so you may want to consider moving outside or evacuating. Temporary shelters are also very useful if you need to evacuate, but you have to do it on foot.

Temporary shelters can be made from tarps and pieces of scrap. Tents make a good shelter if you have one, but practice putting it up before you end up in a disaster. It is also a good idea to practice pitching a tent or setting up an emergency shelter in the dark. You can use a vehicle for a temporary shelter even if it is out of gas.

The choice you make will depend on many things. If you have animals, you may prefer to stay close to home, so you can continue to care for them. However, if you are caring for an elderly or disabled person in your family, you may need a more standard location. Keep in mind that tents and other temporary structures put you in a very vulnerable situation when it comes to looters.

If you must move out of your house and want to set up a temporary shelter, you will need to move your stores outside as quickly as possible. You will also need clothing that will protect you from the weather. For the shelter, you will need these items:

- Lightweight tent (you may need several depending on your family size and the amount of your stored items.
- 15' nylon cord to act as clothesline
- Locks that will fit your tent
- Ax
- Small cook stove with fuel
- A thick bottomed pot and pan
- Paper tableware

Tents should be set up before a disaster strikes. They should also have all their seams sealed once a year.

Planning your escape route

Before any disaster strikes, you should have several escape routes planned out of your area. You should also plan where you could spend the night that is far enough away from your area, but within range of a half tank of gas. You should plan on traveling a minimum of fifty miles away.

What is an emergency shelter?

You family or friends should always be your first option for alternate shelter during a disaster. However, there are plenty of private and public shelters set up for people to use as an emergency shelter. Private shelters are held in churches or clubs (like the VFW) and should be considered as a second choice. They hold fewer people and most of them are going to be friends. If you have no other options, you can go to a government designed public evacuation place. These provide a roof over your head, but are not very secure.

You cannot bring alcohol or weapons to an emergency shelter. When you first arrive at a shelter, you will need to check-in, and you should tell those running the shelter if you have valuable skills they could use. The people in charge of the shelter are often overburdened, so volunteer where you can to help ease their burden and make the shelter run more smoothly. After you have settled in, be sure to read the rules to your entire family, so everyone knows what is expected.

If you have to use an emergency shelter, keep your stuff and your children with you at all times, and do not let other people see what items you are carrying. Make sure an adult is always awake and watching over those who are sleeping. It may help to band together with other people and form a mini-community. Bring coloring books, puzzles, and games to keep your kids quiet and occupied. Do not play loud music or cause disruptions.

You also might want to consider renting a storage place for most of your items and a P.O. Box for mail. Pets are not allowed in these shelters, but there may be a special shelter for pets nearby.

What do I take with me if I am told to evacuate?

If you are limited by time and can only take what you can carry, grab the first two items on the list. If you can take your vehicle, take items in this order:

First – take your basic survival kit (bug out bag). Second – take all the cash you have and any valuables and weapons (weapons will not be allowed if you are evacuating to an emergency shelter). Third – take one week worth of clothing. Finally – if there is room fill your vehicle with any food and potable water you have stored.

Returning to your home after an evacuation

At some point, authorities will clear the area, and you will be allowed back to your home after evacuating. When this happens, it is imperative you enter your home with caution. One person should go into the home to check it out first. Have the rest of your family stay outside at a safe distance from the home. Before you turn any lights on, use your flashlight to thoroughly inspect your home for damage – especially damage to electrical wires and gas lines. If everything looks okay and there is not a smell of gas or any other noticeable hazards, you may turn on the lights, but keep damaged utilities shut off until a professional can check them. Clean up any spills that occurred. Once you home is secure, have your family come inside and begin unloading your stuff. Call your out of state contact to let him or her know you have returned home, and you are okay. Check on your neighbors to see if any of them were unable to evacuate and are now in need of help.

Part V: Specific Natural Disaster Preparation

Chapter 18: Earthquakes

What is an earthquake?

The earth's surface likes to be in constant motion. Sometimes the movement of the different plates on the surface of the earth gets stuck. When they get unstuck, it causes an earthquake. The things we build, such as homes, bridges, and roads, are not always able to withstand this sudden movement. If the stress on the structure becomes too great, it will completely collapse.

Preparing your home and possessions for an earthquake

Do not hang items over sleeping areas. Heavy items, like furnaces, should be attached to wall studs with bolts or metal straps. Installing child locks on cabinets will keep items inside them if an earthquake strikes. You should store heavy items on the lowest shelves.

If you live in an area that receives frequent earthquakes, you may want to have a contractor check your home and make recommendations about structural changes that might improve the stability of your home during an earthquake. You should also have an automatic gas shut-off valve installed that closes when triggered by earthquake vibrations.

Whether you live in an earthquake zone or not, practice earthquake drills with your family. Earthquakes can technically occur anywhere on the earth's surface.

What should I do if I am outside or driving during an earthquake?

If you are driving, pull over to the side of the road at the first sign of any noticeable earth movement. Try to stop at least fifty feet from bridges, buildings, trees, signs, power lines and towers. You must stay inside your car. After an earthquake, drive carefully, because there may be structural damage to bridges, roadways, and overpasses.

If you are outside, sit down on the ground. Try to stay at least fifty feet away from anything that might fall like large signs, bridges, trees, or buildings.

What do I do if I am inside during an earthquake?

Get to the closest safe place, squat down, and cover your head. A safe place is underneath a heavy desk, well build bed, a table, or any other heavy furniture that can give you protection. If there is no safe place in the room, get into a corner away from windows, mirrors, and outer walls. Do not try to go in or out of a building and do not use elevators.

If I get trapped by debris, how do I survive?

If you become trapped under debris, cover your mouth with a piece of cloth to keep dust out of your lungs. Bang on something or whistle, but do not yell unless you hear rescuers calling for you and you have no other way to signal them. Do not light a lighter or a match. Gas lines break

Surviving after the earthquake

After the initial earthquake there will be aftershocks, although these will not be as strong, they can still collapse already damaged structures and cause further damage. Do not attempt to use the roads. Check on neighbors and any elderly people living on your street to make sure they have not become trapped in their homes. Only use the phone in an emergency; allow your out-of-state contact person to let others know about your safety. Listen and smell for the scent of gas in your home to determine if it is safe; if you suspect a gas leak never use the phone inside your home as it could trigger an explosion. Assume all water from the tap is non-potable unless told otherwise. Remember that animals can become aggressive after earthquakes.

Chapter 19: Tsunamis

What is a tsunami?

When earthquakes occur along the ocean floor, giant tidal waves are released, called tsunamis. Tsunamis can be very dangerous and affect areas up to a mile away from the sea coast and up to twenty-five feet above sea level. There is usually very little warning, but if you are at the beach and see water receding toward the sea, you should get as far away as possible.

How to prevent yourself from becoming a tsunami victim

The best way to prevent yourself from becoming a victim of a tsunami is to evacuate with your survival pack as soon as you know one is coming. Make sure you head for higher ground.

Surviving after the tsunami

After a tsunami, do not return to the areas that are flooded until you are given the okay by officials. The water that is left after a tsunami can be contaminated for a long time, making people who are exposed to it sick.

Chapter 20: Volcanoes

What causes volcanic eruptions?

Volcanoes are created by weak spots in the earth's surface (or crust). Usually many things occur before a volcano will erupt, but some are not monitored in all volcanic areas. And others, like movements and mass failures, occur immediately before the volcano erupts. It is never a good idea to live close to a volcano, even a dormant one. If a volcano is nearby, be sure to listen for any warnings that scientists give about future activity.

Tremors and earthquakes are the most widespread measure of whether a volcano is "waking up." The ground around some volcanoes seems to be moving constantly. However, for others, it only begins to move when they are preparing to erupt. The increase in seismic activity seems to be a good predictor. Most of the activity is not strong enough to be measured without special equipment, so do not expect that you will feel an earthquake before it erupts.

Other methods used to monitor volcanoes and predict eruptions are: sulfur dioxide emissions (an increase or decrease in normal activity), ground deformation (a bulge or swell in the shape of a volcano), thermal changes on the surface (measured through infrared), hydrology (looking at sediments), remote sensing (using satellites to predict with electromagnetic energy), monitoring other land movements (like mud slides or lahars). Some people have also predicted volcanic eruptions by monitoring connected volcanoes, monitoring below ground magma activity, and watching for changes in groundwater around the volcano.

How to prepare for a volcanic eruption

If you live close to a volcano, the best preparation is to have your basic survival kit ready in your evacuation vehicle at all times. Always park with your vehicle facing the road and keep the tank at least half full.

Keep evacuation routes with current hazard zone maps in the vehicle that are easily accessible for the driver.

Pyroclastic flow rates are over 400 mph and have temperatures over 1000 degrees Fahrenheit. If you feel an unusual earthquake, see a large amount of smoke and ash, or have any advanced warning of a potential eruption, do not wait to see if it will happen, just leave. This may make for some unnecessary trips and false alarms, but it is better than the alternative.

If you live near a volcano but not in the immediate danger zone, you are a little safer. For there is no danger of being hit by anything the volcano spews at you. You need to prepare for the eminent shut down that will occur after the eruption. Aside from the basic survival kit and a month of potable water, you might want to invest in respirators and special ventilation for your safe room. Gases from the volcano are deadly.

Hazards after the eruption

Eruptions can last for days; stay inside until everything has settled down. Even after the eruption, you may be asked to evacuate. Listen to the radio to keep posted about new developments. Do not drink water from the tap or from wells unless you have been told it is safe.

Chapter 21: Floods

Preparing for a flood

The first thing you should do to prepare for a flood is ensure that you have flood insurance. Standard insurance policies do not necessarily cover flooding. There is government flood insurance available for a reasonable price as long as you do not live in a flood zone. It is only available through certain agents, so you would need to do research in order to purchase it.

Keep records, photographs, and valuables in a separate, secure location like a bank that is not located in a flood zone. Install check valves in your sewer line to prevent water from backing up and flooding your drains. Make sure you keep enough potable water stored for you and your family to drink. Water sources become contaminated when flooding occurs. Keep large valuable items on upper floors if you live in a flood zone.

If a flood watch is issued, make sure your gas tank is full and your car has your basic survival kits loaded in it. Keep watching or listening to the news so you are constantly aware of the situation. Do not allow yourself to be cut off.

Travelling during a flood

Plan your flood evacuation route through high-ground to minimize the chance of being cut-off. If you are concerned that your evacuation route may be blocked because of flooding, do not hesitate to leave before it does. Stay well clear of downed power lines. Water conducts electricity. Never drive through flooded roads. The roadway could be washed away and pits or sinkholes could trap your vehicle in rising water.

Wear heavy rubber boots when evacuating in case you need to abandon your vehicle. If water rises around your vehicle, escape to higher ground immediately. One to two feet of water is enough to sweep your vehicle along with it. Avoid walking through moving water. Even shallow streams can take an adult with them.

Do-it-yourself floatation devices

If you live in an area prone to floods, it is recommended that you not only learn how to swim, but that you also keep personal floatation devices in your home and put them on if flooding occurs. Type II and type III personal floatation devices bought in a store will keep your head out of the water even if you are unconscious. In addition, their bright orange color will make you easier to find in murky waters. A self-inflating raft is also a valuable investment.

If you find yourself in a situation where flood waters are rising and they caught you without these devices, you can make your own floatation raft by screwing lids on milk jugs and tying them together.

If you find yourself in water without a floatation device, you can use your own clothing to keep you afloat. By taking off your pants, knotting the legs, filling them with air, and sealing the waist as best you can, they can act as a device to keep you afloat. You can also use your shirt, coat, or other article of clothing in a similar manner. You must be able to tread water while you are making the device, but it will help you stay afloat in turbid waters with less effort. Air will eventually leak out of clothing, so make sure you refill them when they get low. Also, taking your clothing off can increase your chances of hypothermia in colder waters. Be sure to balance between how much warmth you need and how much added floatation you need.

Surviving after a flood

Even when the flood is receding, well water and city water remain unsafe to drink. Do not drink water from your tap until it has been tested and is safe. Standing water can be hazardous because it may contain raw sewage or be electrically charged. It is best to stay clear of it. Buildings that have been flooded could also be unsafe. Have a licensed contractor look at them to ensure there is no foundational or structural damage before entering them.

If you evacuated from a flooded area, do not return to your home until you are told it is safe by local authorities. When you return, clean and disinfect everything that the water touched. Fabric and cloth items can be washed in a strong detergent and dried on high or in the sun. Colorfast items can be cleaned using the bleach disinfectant described in Chapter 13. Non-colorfast items can be sprayed with Lysol. Allow all items to sit in the sun will be beneficial.

Chapter 22: Weather Related Disasters

Surviving a heat wave

When it is hot outside, we need to keep our bodies cool. Our bodies sweat to cool themselves, but if we do not drink enough water, they will not be able to cool themselves. The most important thing to do to survive a heat wave is to drink water continuously. Electrolyte solutions can prevent your body from losing vital minerals and are okay to drink, but stay away from hydrating yourself with caffeinated beverages and alcohol. If you do not have air conditioning or if your power goes out and you can no longer air condition your home, consider visiting a public building that does have it. If this is not an option, consider putting your swimsuits on and taking turns relaxing in a cold bath tub. You body loses heat much faster when it is immersed in water.

Protect your skin by wearing sunscreen with an SPF of 15 or higher. Wrap a wet towel on your head and then place a wide-brimmed hat over that. Do not do strenuous activity when it is hot. Keep extra water in your car and never leave children or animals in a sealed vehicle.

Surviving a blizzard

Your best chance for surviving a blizzard is to be prepared enough before one is announced. Evacuating is not a good option because you could end up stranded in your car during the blizzard. If a blizzard is coming your way, make sure you have enough food and water stored to last at least two weeks. Stores will probably be packed and supplies low, so hopefully you will have already stockpiled this. Also, you will need your all your survival kits, a shovel, and snow melt (a couple of bags of water softener salt will also work). You should also have layers of weather appropriate clothing, such as coats, snow pants, boots, scarves, and gloves. Ask a doctor for an extra prescription or samples so that you have enough to last you through two weeks. Do not make a run for supplies immediately before a blizzard hits because you may get stuck out in it.

During the blizzard if your heat goes out, find a small interior room and keep your family together there. Share blankets and pack on layers of clothing. If your electric goes out, you can store food outside, but try to open doors as little as possible. If you do not have medical problems, clear the snow from your sidewalk and fire hydrants each day or up to three times a day to keep it from building up and make the job quicker. Never stay outside for more than fifteen minutes at a time and tie a rope to your house and yourself if visibility is low. Drink a warm drink like hot tea or hot chocolate before and after going outside. Do not drink alcohol before going outside. Alcohol makes you feel warmer by relaxing your blood vessels, which in turn cools your inner core sooner.

In order to treat frostbite (white, tingling extremities), place the body part in lukewarm water, or for quicker results place your affected extremity on someone else's stomach (get their permission first). When the blizzard is finished, check on your neighbors especially the elderly.

Surviving a hurricane

If you live along the coast or a waterway where a hurricane is likely to strike, the first thing you should do is review your insurance policy and make sure you have flood insurance. After you have confirmed or purchased flood insurance, you will want to invest in storm shutters or at the minimum ½" exterior grade plywood. If you choose the option of plywood, install bolts or other permanent attachment links around your windows, cut the plywood to fit each window, paint or stain it to protect it from rotting, and mark which window it goes on with a permanent marker. Keep a box of nuts and washers on hand so you do not have to worry about running out when a storm is approaching. It is an excellent idea to create a safe room if you are planning on waiting out any hurricanes you can. The safe room should be on the top floor of your home and you should have brightly colored inflatable rafts, lifejackets, an ax, and a handsaw available in case flood waters rise too high. Create an evacuation plan that will take you fifty miles or more inland and allow you to stay with your pets (if you have any). Keep your gutters and downspouts clean.

When a hurricane watch is issued, you should eat as many of your perishables as you can. Turning your refrigerator and freezer to low will help preserve what is left as long as possible if the power goes out. Secure your windows and cover with prepared plywood. Fill your tubs and sinks with water before it is contaminated, so you will have extra. Also, you can shock your pool if you have one, which should make it easier to clean when the storm is done. However, do not lower the water level in your pool. You should also secure any outdoor items and bring them inside if possible. Listen or watch the news and if you are told to evacuate do it, and if you are told to shut off your utilities, do it. You should also turn off your utilities and evacuate if you are not well stocked, if you are nervous about staying, if you rely on power for health reasons, if you live near water, or if you live in a structure such as a mobile home that does not weather storms well.

If you decide to stay during the hurricane, remain inside even during the eye of the storm (or calm part), Move to your safe room and watch the news.

After the storm, be careful if you go outside. Animals move to higher ground and you may find testy animals in unusual places. Open your windows and doors to air your house. Do not drink the tap water until you are told it is safe. If your pool has become contaminated with saltwater, you will need to call your service company for instructions on cleaning it.

Surviving a tornado, cyclone, or twister

You will have little, if any, advanced warning of a tornado. Sometimes it is very calm right before they hit. Sometimes the sky will turn the shade of the green Caribbean Sea. Once a tornado watch is issued, you should get your survival pack on your back and your whistle around your neck. You can bring in outdoor furniture, but take your radio with you and keep checking the sky. If a warning is issued, get to a safe place immediately. A corner in the basement or a root cellar is the best places. Abandon your trailer or mobile home and lay down in a ditch outside in a large open area.

After the tornado has passed, call the police and let them know where it was. Be sure to smell and listen for gas leaks. Do not use any appliances indoors, leave the house, and shut off the gas if you think it is leaking. You should call the gas company from a safe distance away. Check neighbors, especially older people, but be aware of structural damage. Do not go into an unsafe home, or you may need to be rescued as well.

Part VI: Disasters That Originate From Both Human and Natural Causes

Chapter 23: EMPs

What is an EMP?

An EMP or electromagnetic pulse is an explosion of electromagnetic radiation. Although the EMP does not kill people, it targets electrical lines, circuits, and transformers and ruins them. It creates a fluctuating magnetic field that causes a surge in electrical flow and voltages. Do not expect to be able to use your radio, car, computer, television, or telephone (even if it is an old plug in type).

EMPs caused by solar flares

EMPs and their destructive power were first associated with solar flares. A solar flare is when part of the sun's surface gives off intense light and a cloud of heavy isotopes, electrons, and atoms are released. The flare is powered by a release of magnetic energy. When this magnetic energy is in the X-ray and UV ray range, it may cause communication problems, especially with long range radio communication. It also can affect radar. When a large solar flare is released, it can create an EMP that will lock on to the power grid and destroy it. Although a strong solar flare occurred in 2003, the last time there was a solar flare strong enough to wipe out the grid occurred in 1859. At that time, there was only a minimal grid of telegraph wires, but these were affected and had to be repaired. Solar flares cannot be predicted as of yet.

HEMPs

With the invention of nuclear weapons, a new way of generating EMPs that affected large areas was discovered. Although nuclear weapons that are detonated on the ground have an EMP associated with them, these are limited to the area of the atomic blast. When the first test bombs were exploded, the equipment measuring the blasts was shielded from the predicted EMP, but some of it was still wrecked. As the experiments grew, nuclear bombs were tested at high altitudes. When this happened, the EMP combined with the earth's magnetic field, increased the range. These are called HEMPs. It is estimated that one nuclear blast occurring 250 miles above Kansas could destroy electronics across the entire United States.

EMP Generators

Since the discovery of the destructive power of EMPs in 1962, countries have developed ways of creating them without the nuclear blast. At this time, the non-nuclear EMP or NNEMP is not as far reaching as either one caused by an intense solar flare or HEMP, because it is created with a controlled chemical reaction. However, the area that it hits would still be as devastated.

How to survive an EMP

The primary survival techniques for an EMP are identical to those for a power outage with extra things to take into consideration. First, with a power outage, the power is usually restored after power lines are repaired by weaving broken ones back together. However, with an EMP blast, the circuits and the computers controlling those circuits would be destroyed and need to be rebuilt. Although magnetic shielding is available, only companies (and individuals) that had enough of it in place before the EMP would be safe. Because the recovery from an EMP would take much longer, you would need to prepare ways to live long term by having a way to raise or hunt food. Second, you will probably not have a vehicle, a way of communicating (although older HAM radios and things powered by vacuum tubes will theoretically work), or a working generator.

Chapter 24: Wildfires and House Fires

Protecting your home from wildfires

The best way to protect your home from wildfires is to keep your yard well groomed and keep brush, bushes, and trees thirty feet away from your home. Consider only using vegetation that is fire-resistant. If you have firewood, stack it thirty feet away from your house. Wooden structures such as fences and sheds, flammable materials such as gasoline, and outbuildings should also follow the thirty foot rule.

Make sure your home and street signs are easy to read so firefighters and other emergency workers can find you. Make sure that they have access to water sources, such as swimming pools and fire hydrants.

Install working fireproof shutters to protect your windows. Get covers for vents and eaves that prevent sparks from entering.

Evacuation

When you are warned that a wildfire is in the area, it is important to evacuate immediately. Wildfires are not predictable and travel rapidly. It is easier to prepare your house and leave if you listen to the first call to evacuate. Before preparing your house, pack your vehicle and place any pets where you can easily grab them. Have your car facing the street.

To prepare your house, you should shut off the gas and propane tanks; you will need to pay a professional to turn it back on. Take any gas grills and other flammable items thirty feet away from your home. Shut all windows, vents, and interior doors. Move your furniture to the center of each room. If you have curtains that are not fire-resistant, take them down. Open the damper for your fireplace if you have one, but make sure the spark screen is in place. Finally, connect all the sprinklers you have and turn them on so they continuously water your house, roof and the lawn around them.

Know several evacuation routes and take the one that is traveling away from the fire. Keep the news on so that you can hear if the fire changes directions and be prepared to change direction if needed. If you are trapped in an area with a wildfire, be sure to find a body of water – pools, streams, lakes, etc. – and submerge yourself in it as deep as you can. Get a cloth or wet your shirt and cover your face and mouth with it to protect them from the heat.

What to do if you catch on fire.

If you catch on fire, the first thing you may feel is like it is happening to someone else and you are watching. In some cases, it may be difficult to stop what you are doing, get down on the ground, and roll with your hands over your face to put the flames out. Choking the oxygen from the fire is the quickest way to eliminate it.

If you see someone who is on fire, cover them with a blanket, help them lay on the floor, and roll them until the flames are out.

Preventing Fire in Your Home

In addition to being prepared for wildfires, you should try to prevent fires that start in the home. There are several fires safety measures you should be following before a fire strikes. First, you need to have fire alarms on every floor and near bedrooms and kitchens. Teach your children never to play with fire, the stove, or matches and then keep all items that could cause a fire out of the reach of your children. Be sure to practice fire drills three or four times a year and have the children alternate between two different ways out. Everyone should know two ways to evacuate from each room in your house. Schedule a time for your children to visit a firehouse and see a firefighter in full dress. Explain to them that they should not be afraid and should go to firefighters if they are trapped in a fire.

Kitchens are one of the main places where a fire can start in any household. If you purchase a fire extinguisher for you kitchen, make sure it is rated "ABC" to put out fires. Turn the handles on your pots and pans away from the front of the stove, and keep anything that could catch fire away from it. This includes piles of napkins or other flammable items that may be stored near it or on the back of the counter. If a fire occurs on the stove while you are cooking and you do not have a fire extinguisher, you can either cover the pot with a lid to choke the fire, or if the fire has spread beyond the pot, you can dump a box of baking soda on it. For this reason, you should always keep an open box near your stove (not stored over the stove).

The furnace, hot water heater, woodstove, fireplace, washer, and dryer areas are other fire hazard places. Do not store anything that could catch on fire near to these items. All major appliances that use flames or heat should be installed and vented properly. Make sure you have a chimney sweep clean and inspect your chimney each year. Also, always make sure the lint trap is clean before drying a load of clothes. Once a year, you should check the dryer vent and the hose leading to it for lint build-up and remove any you find. Never dry anything that was used to absorb solvents.

Around the house, check all plugs and cords to make sure they are in good repair. Do not run cords under rugs or carpets and not to staple or nail them in place. Be careful that doors can open and close freely without crushing cords. Do not fill outlets with more items than they are designed to hold. Unused outlets should be covered with plug covers even if there are no small children in the house to prevent accidents. Small appliances should be unplugged whenever they are not being used.

Outside, always make sure that any fire hydrants on your property are clean, easily accessed, and free of brush or snow. Your house needs to have clear numbers that are visible from the street. It is a good idea to have your house numbers painted on your curb, as well as on your mailbox, and your house itself.

What to do if your home catches on fire

Small grease fires can be put out quickly by throwing baking soda on them or placing a lid over them (if they are in a pan or pot). You can use a fire extinguisher on fires that are a little larger, call 911 or send someone to do it. For larger fires, you need to evacuate immediately and then call 911 from a safe distance.

If you are trapped in a closed room during a fire, feel the door before opening it. Doors will keep fire out for a little while. Never open a hot door because fire is on the other side of it. When moving through a burning home to evacuate, cover your nose and mouth with a rag if possible. Crawl on the floor and keep your head low where the air is fresher.

It is vital to remember that you should never go back into a burning building. Fire fighters have special equipment and special training. They will take care of the situation when they arrive in the best way possible.

Chapter 25: Pandemic

What is a pandemic?

Bacteria easily exchange antibiotic resistance between each other, and viral diseases have no cure. Although we have more advanced medicines available to us than what we had in the early 1900's, we still need to be aware that a pandemic is just as possible today as it was years ago.

A disease that remains local and perhaps only affects your family or a few others is simply said to be "going around." Sometimes, diseases become more serious and spread quickly through larger populations. These are called epidemics. When an epidemic reaches the global level, it is called a pandemic.

Although traditional pandemics cause rapid, large-scale death, AIDS is considered a very active pandemic today. It does not kill quickly, but it affects a large number of people across several continents.

If a disastrous pandemic were to occur in the world, it would probably be a form of the flu (such as SARS or swine flu), Ebola, smallpox (if it were revived or escaped one of the labs that contain it), or even something like the bubonic plague. Pandemics can occur naturally, or they could be inadvertently caused by a biological weapon.

How can you protect yourself and your loved ones?

Some disasters are short lived. The danger comes and goes and then you can carry on with your normal day to day life while the world around you recovers. Pandemics are an entirely different story. When a pandemic hits, you will need to stay in your safe room a minimum of ten days and perhaps up to thirty days. Pandemics are probably the only disaster that those who are capable of safely stockpiling the most stores will be in the best position to survive. Although medicines and vaccines can be administered to help reduce the length of time of the pandemic, it will still take time to stop it spread and reduce the number of infected people.

N95 masks are very important should you have to deal with a pandemic. These face masks will filter out 95% of all biological pathogens. There are also N100 face masks that filter out 99.9% of all pathogens. Either of these is a good stock item to have on hand. Make sure you know if your mask is reusable or if it is for a one time use.

To reduce the chances of getting sick, you need to include hand washing as a part of your daily regimen. While hand sanitizers are important, you need to try to wash your hands with soap and water as well, especially if you have been outside. Unless the pandemic was caused by a terrorist attack on the water supply, you should have access to potable water. Wash your hands before you eat, after you use the restroom, after you deal with any sick people, and especially before you touch any part of your face.

As an additional preventative measure, make sure you keep any open wounds covered. You should be sure to get more sleep and take a multivitamin.

How to avoid spreading pandemics

The best way to prevent the spread of a pandemic is to stay home. Many years ago, when the bubonic plague was passing through the Middle East, a man locked himself and his family inside his home until the danger had passed. No one in his home was infected, and they all lived to tell the story.

In some cases, you may share living quarters with other people (such as in apartments) and this will not be as effective. In that case, you may want to invest in a "Bubble" style safe room that will inflate in time of pandemic. These kinds of safe room come with backup power sources designed to keep filtering air for a long time (including manual pumps). Although they are expensive, you may even want two of them, in case one of your family members becomes sick – then you can quarantine him or her in a protective bubble.

Wearing a face mask designed to keep out disease is also important to prevent the spread of a pandemic. You should pay careful attention to sanitation and to washing your hands.

Part VII: Specific Man-made Disaster Preparation

Chapter 26: Chemical and Hazardous Material Spills

What causes a hazardous material spill?

Hazardous material spills occur when they are transported from one place to another place. During transport, human error that leads to an accident can cause the materials to be released into the environment, contaminating all the surrounding areas with deadly chemicals.

Because these occur as the result of an accident, there is no way to predict or pre-warn people about their occurrence.

How do I prepare for a spill?

Be sure to keep 6 mil or thicker plastic on hand, scissors, and plenty of duct tape. These items will help you to seal any windows and doors in your safe room. You should also maintain your other survival supplies.

A safe room or "bubble" with an upgraded ventilation system is also very helpful in protecting you and your family from a chemical or hazardous materials spill.

What do I do after a hazardous material spill?

Once you have been notified there has been a hazardous spill in your area, you need to follow the instructions of the authorities and either evacuate immediately with your basic survival kit, or go to a safe room.

If you are instructed to shelter in your home, be sure you shut off all the heating and air conditioning and close all ventilation. Get your family inside your safe room (preferably located on a second floor) and seal it by covering all the windows and doors with plastic. Turn on the radio and listen for further instructions.

If you are instructed to evacuate, try to follow a route that is upwind of the spill. Turn your heater/ air conditioning unit so that the air in the car is re-circulated and close all windows. Do not get out of your vehicle, and do not return home until authorities instruct you that it is safe to do so.

Chapter 27: Nuclear Accidents

What causes nuclear accidents?

Nuclear accidents are caused by the meltdown of a nuclear power plant or a terrorist attack on a nuclear power plant. Attacks by nuclear weapons or dirty bombs are dealt with specifically under the terrorism chapter.

Making electricity with nuclear power generates a great deal of heat. This heat is usually controlled through a series of cooling systems. However, when the plant malfunctions because of human or mechanical error, temperatures can rise causing the plant to meltdown and release radiation into the surrounding areas. In some cases, other disasters, like earthquakes, can lead to power plant malfunctions and meltdowns.

What are the hazards of a nuclear accident?

Radioactive isotopes are the main danger for a nuclear accident. Radioactive iodine is particularly hazardous. Because of this, you should keep a radiation detector in your home and learn how to use it. Some radiation detectors measure the accumulation of radiation and others measure the current radiation.

Radiation can affect food and water stores. It is important to not eat or drink anything that has not been stored in a sealed glass, plastic, or metal container. You should wash the tops of cans with 1 cup bleach to 10 cups water solution before opening them. You should also use this solution to wash any eating utensils that have not been stored in a sealed container before using them.

Another hazard of a nuclear accident is clothing contamination. If you are outside or in an area where you could have been exposed to radiation, you need to come home, cut your clothing off, seal it in a plastic bag, throw it away outside of the house, and take a long shower.

You can use the bleach solution and blot your skin before showering as an added precaution. It is helpful to store a few changes of clothes in a plastic container at home, so you have uncontaminated clothing in case one of these disasters occurs near your home.

You should have enough stored in your safe room to survive for a minimum of 8 – 12 hours after a nuclear accident. Keep your radio on and follow any directions given.

How to survive after a nuclear accident

Everyone living within 10 miles of a nuclear power plant will receive yearly information from emergency officials that is filled with nuclear accident survival information specific to your area. You should review this information with your family and keep it in your safe room.

You can take potassium iodide (if you have some on hand) to help prevent against radiation damage to your thyroid, but you should only take them if you are told to by the authorities. Not all leaks contain iodine atoms. Although this tablet can be very beneficial if taken when told to do it, too much iodine is not good for your body. Also be aware that you should not use iodine to purify water while taking potassium iodine tablets to prevent radiation poisoning.

If you are told to shelter in home, close all doors and windows. Seal your safe room with plastic in the same way you would for a chemical or hazardous materials spill. Close vents, shut off ventilation, heating, and cooling systems. Do not use the phone unless it is an emergency. Stay in your safe room until you are told it is safe to come out of it.

If you are told to evacuate the area, you need to leave immediately. Grab your bug-out bags and a few sources of entertainment for your children. Stay on the evacuation route the officials have told you to use. Other routes may have higher levels of radiation on them. If you have a radiation detector, bring it with you.

Chapter 28: Terrorism

What should I expect if a terrorist attacks?

Terrorism is the basest form of guerilla warfare. Terrorists use homemade or illegally obtained weapons in order to kill as many people as possible for their cause. For a while, terrorism in the United States was primarily carried out through plane hijacking and taking hostages. However, bombs have been the traditional method for terrorists to do their damage. A few American terrorists, such as the "Unabomber" have also used bombs throughout their careers.

There are three different types of bombs that terrorists use – biological weapons, chemical weapons, and dirty bombs. Each one has its own destructive factors. Some are contained to specific areas and others can become widespread. Some cause instant death and others may just make you sick.

Whenever and however terrorists strike, the effects are usually devastating. It is important to pay attention to what is going on around you and be prepared if terrorists attack. Never accept a package from an unknown sender – especially if there is no return address on it.

What should I do if I am taken hostage?

Obviously, no one wants to ever be a hostage for any reason. Being aware of your surrounding can play a key role in whether or not you become one. If you are in a public place and you see something that looks like it may develop into a hostage situation, do not stick around and watch like many people do. Whenever you are faced with a situation that is rapidly becoming volatile, your first thought should be escape. Watch it safely from your own home on the news in the evening.

If you cannot escape, your next choice should be to stay where you are with your head down. If, for example, you are on a cruise ship that has been taken over, but there are no terrorists in your area, go to your room, shut and lock the door, turn off the lights, and shut off your cell phone but put it on the charger. You may want to fill as many containers as you can with water because you may spend several days in your room like this. Windows, and even walls, can be dangerous, so keep yourself away from them as much as possible.

If you are actually captured as a hostage, you may first be alarmed, but eventually you will accept your situation. The people who are most likely to survive have a positive attitude and have faith in something (even if it is only faith that you will be rescued). Another important thing to remember in case you are taken hostage is: do not resist. Also, do not ever make eye contact with your captors. You should, however, act calm and resigned – not subservient. Understand that there may be times you will have to deal with being alone or confined in small places. You may also end up losing track of time. Just keep your positive attitude.

At some point, you may be allowed to talk. If you are given this luxury, never argue. You can tell your captors about your life and your family. You can ask you captors about their lives and families. As long as you do not argue and remain positive but non-challenging, you should be fine. Know that whether you talk to your captors or not the next stage you will enter is the accommodation stage. You may become very bored or very afraid. You may become exhausted and even without talking to the terrorists you may begin to identify with them. All of these emotions are normal and have been felt by hostages before you. Many hostages find it easier to get through this stage if they have a visual image they can draw upon. Go to a familiar place in your head and imaging you are spending an entire day there. Complete a difficult task in your head like building a race car from scratch or knitting a baby layette and then the rest of the clothing as a child develops. Your primary focus should be on surviving, but you should maintain your sense of humor.

Eventually, you will be rescued. The key to being rescued is to keep your blindfold on if you have one. Once you realize you are being rescued, you should get down and stay low. You could take cover in a bed or in a bathtub, but keep your hands out where they can be seen.

You want your rescuers to know that you are not a terrorist. Even if you are being rescued, you should remain as you are so the rescuers can finish taking care of the situation. Once it is clear, they will tell you to get up. Try to remember who captured you and what they look like. In some circumstances, terrorists have tried to walk out with the hostages, being able to identify them will ensure justice is served.

Once you are rescued, you will need to learn coping and resolution strategies. It is good to find a counselor or a psychologist to help work through your ordeal.

What to do after an explosion

Because terrorists frequently use bombs, you should know what to do when one goes off nearby. If the explosion traps you, you need to remain calm and lie still. Cover your nose and mouth with a cloth. Do not shout for help unless you hear rescuers calling to you. Bang on a pipe to draw attention to your location instead.

If an explosion goes off when you are in a building, and you are not trapped, get out of the building as quickly and calmly as possible. Once you are in a safe place, you need to write down everything you remember happening and people you remember seeing both before and after the event.

What is a radiological dispersion device?

An RDD (radiological dispersion device) or dirty bomb is either a small, portable nuclear bomb or a bomb that has been contaminated with radioactive material. These nuclear weapons will only affect a relatively small area, but they will do a great amount of damage on that area. If an explosion goes off near you, always suspect it is a dirty bomb. Cover your nose and mouth to prevent radioactive particles from entering your body.

In a full-fledged nuclear attack, where the affected area is large, you would want to find immediate close shelter. If you were outside, you would want to lie flat on the ground behind a hill or rise covering your eyes until the blast and the shockwave pass over you. Resist the urge to look at a nuclear blast. Watching it without special eye protection will blind you. After the blast is finished, you would want to find the closest place to remove your clothing and shower (which may be a decontamination station set up by the government). If you are inside or near a building, you would want to get in the basement or innermost room and seal it. Remember, nuclear blasts cause EMP pulses, so you may have trouble with vehicles and communication. In general, the same directions you would follow for a nuclear meltdown are applicable to a nuclear bomb. The main exception is that potassium iodide would not be beneficial in the case of nuclear weapons. A N95 or better face mask not only protects against biological hazards, but it also protects against radiation as well.

RDDs, on the other hand, are extremely different from a nuclear meltdown or a full-fledged nuclear bomb. While all nuclear weapons have an EMP associated with them, those from dirty bombs affect a very small area. Even if the bomb is one of the backpack nuclear weapons unaccounted for from former Soviet Union stockpiles, it would still not be as devastating as a full scale attack. For this reason, when a dirty bomb (or any explosive device) is used, the key to survival is to escape the affected area. Travel upwind; try to put as much space between you and the site of the explosion as quickly as it can. Remember, because speed and distance are key factors, you may need to abandon your vehicle and run on foot if traffic slows or stops.

Once you have escaped the contaminated area, find a place to remove your clothing and shower. You will need clean clothes; it should be safe to purchase them outside of the affected area. You should always cut or tear your clothing off instead of dragging your contaminated clothes over your head. Seal clothing in a plastic bag and throw away. Shampoo your hair twice and be sure to scrub the rest of your body. After you put on your clean clothes, go to the nearest hospital.

What are the symptoms of radiation poisoning?

It takes up to three or four hours before you will begin to feel the effects of radiation poisoning. Try to be at a hospital before they begin. At first you will feel withdrawn and tired, and then you will begin vomiting. You will feel sick anywhere from eight hours to three days.

After you are feeling better, your hair will fall out. Then you will get very sick again between weeks eight and fourteen. Plan to have someone available to take care of you during this time that was not exposed to the radiation.

During the full period of your radiation sickness, you need to get plenty of rest and fluids. Although you will have periods of sickness where you do not feel like doing anything, maintaining high levels of personal hygiene is very important. You also may need antibiotics.

What is a biological weapon?

Biological weapons are weapons created to spread infectious diseases. All of them will make people sick; some of them will cause death. Some may inadvertently cause an epidemic. Because of the widespread effects of biological weapons, countries have agreed to not use them during regular wars, but they are still used by terrorists.

The nature of biological weapons also makes it more difficult for officials to discover what has happened. A pathogen could be released into the system, but until people begin noticing symptoms, the public warning will not be broadcast. Biological weapons can be released into the air, into the food supply, or into the water supply. Biological weapons can be mailed, placed in aerosols, and transmitted person to person.

What are the most common biological weapons?

Any disease could be used to make a biological weapon, but there are a few that are used more regularly or that would make potent candidates. Ebola and other hemorrhagic fevers are probably the top of the list for being lethal. These diseases kill in large numbers.

Smallpox, which was eradicated, is another good candidate for a biological weapon. Smallpox vaccines are no longer used, but vaccination is the only way to prevent contracting the disease. Two laboratories retain experimental samples of the disease, but it could also be re-sequenced.

Anthrax, botulism, tularemia, E. coli, and even the bubonic plague could all be used as biological weapons.

What are the signs and symptoms of exposure?

Most of the pathogens used in biological weapons cause flu-like symptoms, but they can also cause diarrhea.

What is a HEPA filter and how do I manually filter air?

A High-Efficiency Particulate Air filter or HEPA filter filters out pathogens and other air impurities using a fibrous filter system. The filter attracts smaller particles and traps them in its webbing. It uses principles of both airflow and particle collisions.

Official HEPA filters are required to remove 99.97% of all particles 0.3 microns or larger from the air. Some filters will have "HEPA" on them, but add 99%, -like, or other amendments to the designation. These should not be purchased because they may not meet HEPA standards.

HEPA filters do not work on viruses, but they do filter bacteria and radioactive material from the air. You can have a filtration system installed for your safe room. HEPA filters provide protection similar to the N95 or better facial masks. Used in combination, they provide superior defense against biological weapons (or pandemics).

What do I do if a biological weapon has been used?

If you come in contact with a pathogen used in a biological weapon, you need to get away from the source of exposure. Remove your clothing and sanitize them by boiling in water for 30 minutes and then washing. Take a long, soapy shower. See a physician for recommended treatment.

If only some of your family has been exposed to the biological weapon, make sure they are isolated from the rest of the family outside the safe room (or in a separate bubble if you have two). Make sure everyone in the family wears their N95 or better facial masks.

Many of the precautions used for pandemics can be used to help survive a biological weapon attack. For example, it would be a good idea to take a multivitamin. With a biological weapon, the time you have to remain in the safe room should be shorter. It will be easier for government officials to contain and manage this kind of attack since it is on a smaller scale. However, make sure you listen to the news and follow any instructions on obtaining vaccines or other medicines.

What is a chemical attack and which chemicals are used?

A chemical attack is one that uses chemicals instead of a traditional bomb type weapon. They are most dangerous when they are left in enclosed public places. Chemical threats do not just affect people, but also attack animals and plants. The military makes test strips that will warn you if a chemical agent is present.

Typical gases used in a chemical attack are blister agents, blood agents, and nerve agents. Each one affects a different body system. Actual chemicals used are: hydrogen cyanide, cyanogen chloride, mustard gas, Lewisite, phosgene oxime, Tabun, Sarin, Soman, and VX. Of these, cyanogen chloride is unique because it is the only gas that is lighter than air, so it rises. It also will break down the filters in any gas mask. However, nerve gases are the most deadly gases.

How do I survive a chemical attack?

If you are outside when a chemical attack occurs, cover your face, move upwind of the area, and try to get to higher ground (head toward lower ground if you know the gas used was cyanogen chloride). If you are inside, stay inside the building unless the building was the place of the attack. Shut off heating and cooling systems and seal vents.

You can buy gas masks (they are very expensive) and skin decontamination kits (RSDL, M291, M258 in order of newest to oldest). If you purchase a gas mask do not open the filters until you are ready to use them. Open filters only last about 6 months. However, do fit the mask to your face. Men with facial hair will not be able to wear a gas mask, neither will people with respiratory problems.

A safe room for chemical attacks should be located on the second floor. (Do not use it if you know that cyanogen chloride was the chemical used.) Plastic sheet should be ready to attach to all windows and doors. Ideally each person should have about ten square feet of floor space in your safe room. Listen to the news for further instructions. Keep clothing stored in plastic containers in case you are exposed and need to change into clean clothes.

I have been exposed. What do I do now?

If the government has set up a decontamination station, go there with a clean change of clothes sealed in plastic.

If not, 1) use a skin decontamination kit or 2) blot dirt (or flour) over your skin, and use a bleach solution of one cup bleach to ten cups water to blot your skin again.

Cut off your clothing to remove it, place it in a plastic bag, and discard. You should shower, flushing your eyes alone with water for ten minutes (and removing your contacts if you have them). Shampooing your hair twice will help to remove all the chemicals in it. Put on clean clothes that have been stored in a plastic container if your home is in the area of the chemical release. Wash glasses with soapy water, but if they bother your eyes in any way, throw them away.

If you know a nerve gas was involved you will need several shots of atropine. If you have children, they will need a different dosage than an adult dose. Also, make sure you clip the used atropine to yourself.

Chapter 29: Economic Meltdown

What is an economic meltdown?

An economic meltdown is when financial markets crash. The Great Depression, which affected the entire world in one way or another, was a large scale economic meltdown. On an individual country scale, Zimbabwe is a current example of an economic meltdown. Greece could also be considered in an economic meltdown, but the effect of being joined to other European countries has lighted the blow for its people.

At the best, an economic meltdown is minor and only affects a few countries. Japan had a relatively mild economic meltdown during the depression, but its wise Prime Minister averted most of the financial pain for his country until he was assassinated for his efforts.

At worst, an economic meltdown would occur on a global scale and cause the currency in many countries to lose value simultaneously.

What causes an economic meltdown?

Economic meltdown can be sparked by several different things. Greece and Zimbabwe suffer from government corruption that makes it difficult to fix the finances of either country. Germany, after WWI, suffered from immense war payments required because of their part in WWI. The United States suffered from banks that leant out far too much money, when people began to struggle to make payments on their loans; the banks got nervous and called in the loans, which upset the financial balance.

All of these factors can spark the event, but in general, economic meltdowns are caused because of high debt ratios on either a national or personal level.

Warning signs of an economic meltdown

Economic meltdowns begin on a personal level when banks are overgenerous in their lending practices. At some point, the people they are lending to begin to skip payments. In the case of the Great Depression, it was businesses that the banks allowed to have too much money. On a national level, economic meltdowns begin when countries develop more debt than they can handle. In the case of Germany, the country was forced into deep debt from the war, so it began to print money, which increased inflation. A high debt ratio across the population or for a nation is the first warning sign of an economic meltdown.

The next signal is massive default on loans. This can be on a personal scale, when banks begin calling in loans or on a national scale, or on a national scale when governments can no longer pay bills.

At this point, the government will usually step in and do something drastic to help. Sadly, most of these government responses have been based on the theories of John Keynes. Keynes believed that more government debt is good for coming out of economic crisis. This belief still holds even though Germany obviously had more debt than it could handle and Roosevelt ran up more debt during his entire presidency than any other president before him. Why do governments believe more debt is the answer? Some of their belief is based on Japan.

Japan had an economy savvy Prime Minister at the time of the Great Depression. The Prime Minister increased defense spending and ran the country into debt. However, he further devalued the yen. This made imports expensive and increased home production and sales. To counter the inflation that naturally occurred, he set up a system of rations which stabilized prices at home. Unfortunately, as he was bringing Japan about he was assassinated because some people felt they could make more money if he had let the country go into a deeper depression along with the rest of the world.

Keynes claims WWII finally drove the United States in enough debt to pull it out of the depression. Interestingly enough, it was probably the rationing of food that occurred that truly fixed the economy.

Irving Fischer seems to have understood the debt cause better than Keynes, but he is not as popular. This is probably because he seems to encourage fiscal responsibility. He claims that increasing debt ratios eventually leads to reaching the limit. Once the limit is reached, people cannot continue to spend and the market crashes. This creates a scramble for money that destroys the economy. Debts become more difficult to pay because income begins to fall while the cost of the initial debt remains the same.

There are key mistakes a government makes that will lead a nation closer to economic meltdown. The first is freezing wages so that a company cannot cut what they pay people when they are having economic difficulty. This makes a company layoff people it can no longer afford to pay.

The next bad choice a government can make is to increase taxes. Herbert Hoover tried to get away with increasing taxes by reducing the number of exemptions. It makes no difference how a government does it, when taxes go up, unemployment goes up. Businesses that no longer get exemptions try to make their shareholders happy and increase their profits by laying people off.

There are several more things that a government does, which causes harm to their country's economy after it has already started down the path to an economic meltdown. Printing money to pay debts tends to be the favorite approach of governments but devaluing money is a less drastic but better method of handling the problem. Forcing costs of consumer goods to increase by destruction of consumer goods is another bad choice because governments tend not to be good at artificially manipulating markets. Finally, resetting money values shows the country is in bad shape. When inflation is so high the money becomes worthless, the government replaces the old money with new money based on high exchanges for old money. This is a final distress signal. When these factors add up, expect an economic meltdown.

How to prepare for an economic meltdown

The important thing is to not over extend your debt ratio. Some debt is acceptable, but being in debt for more than 30% of your annual income is not. To reduce your debt, cut excess wants from your budget. Get rid of cable and reduce your internet service. Keep enough money and supplies on hand to last at least two weeks in case banks close.

You should also look into gardening and recycling. Raising your own food, especially from seeds that will re-propagate, and preserving your own food are both important ways to keep your family fed when store prices skyrocket and employment is difficult to find. It is also a good idea to buy chickens and perhaps a goat if you have the space. Learn how to raise food now and it will benefit you if the economy collapses.

How to survive an economic meltdown

Since high debt ratios are the path that lead to economic meltdowns, it makes sense that you do not want a high debt ratio going into one. Paradoxically, even with no debt, you must be careful with your investments. The stock market, savings accounts, and even government bond can all become useless over night. It is possible to regain money lost through savings accounts and bonds if the country (and the bank) recovers. Be sure you do your research on the bank you choose and make sure they have strict policies in place that prevent risky loans. Money lost on the stock market will not be recovered, unless you reinvest in companies that will be successful after the crash.

An economic meltdown can take fifteen to twenty years to right itself. Your stockpiles will be useful, but do not use them unless you need them. Ideally, the government will respond by issuing rations. This puts a hold on any internal inflation.

Many jobs will be lost during an economic meltdown. Make sure you have a secure job and seniority. Also, make sure you have skills and goods you can use in barter.

Chapter 30: Cyber War

What is Cyber Warfare?

Since the development of the internet, the world has connected online. The internet was designed so that scholars could share information. Because scholars sharing information rarely sabotage each other, it was never set up with the checks and balances that are necessary to prevent hackers from breaching security.

Fast forward into the future, where not only scholars use the internet, but power companies, banks, and the rest of the population. Not only are the checks and balances absent, but Microsoft's ability to edge out the competition, combined with its need to throw out software before it has been thoroughly tested for security issues, and its vast pocket books that pay governments to look the other way creates serious questions about our cyber safety.

Cyber warfare is when one nation attacks (often without claiming it was on purpose) another nation's online resources. For example, if China would attack the United State's power grid and black out the East Coast – this would be cyber war.

How vulnerable is the United States to attack?
We score high offensively. We could easily attack another nation in new and unusual ways. However, that would require us to make the first move. Because we are so dependent on our computers make us lower than most other nations when it comes to defense. If we are attacked first, we may no longer be able to launch an offensive strike.

Why would Cyber Warfare be Considered a Disaster?

Just as an EMP can knock out computers, a cyber war could not only render our computers useless, it could plant misinformation inside them. If our banks are attacked, we lose all money stored there until the problem is resolved. If our power grid is attacked, we lose all power until it is resolved. And if our Department of Defense is attacked, then we could shot a nuclear weapon at China and get blamed for starting a nuclear war – even though it was the fault of hackers.

Although the chances of starting a nuclear war are far-fetched, there are other acts of war that could be started by knowledgeable hackers and can be blamed on us. A more likely scenario is that they implant a bug in chips destined for all our military planes. After a few months, the chip causes the computer systems to crash, which grounds all our planes and renders us helpless to ward off an open war attack.

Cyber warfare is a real modern threat that could cause a wide scale disaster; it is important to be prepared for it.

How to prepare for and survive a Cyber War

You first thought may be to delete your internet presence and trash your computer. While this would protect your personal computer from being attacked or from being used as a weapon to attack a larger target, it would not prevent the power grid from falling to hackers.

To survive a cyber war, you need to be prepared for the other disasters covered in this book. Cyber war can cause black outs. It can cause massive energy failures. It can cause a nuclear power plant to meltdown. If you are prepared for these disasters, you will also survive a cyber war.

The most devastating cyber attack would be one that targets a bank. In this case, the extra money you keep in your survival kit should help. However, should the bank system be attacked, it would be important not only to have the latest copies of your bank statements but to have a skill or goods you could used to barter. Do you sew? Can you perform electrical work? Do you have a garden where you can raise extra produce? Should the banking community collapse, the more items you have that are valuable from a survival perspective, the better your chances of finding a niche and surviving.

Chapter 31: Conclusion

Look at this guide as the beginning of your disaster knowledge. There are many courses in survival for the wilderness that will help in the case of a disaster. Also, there are groups you can find and join that will improve your survival skills and help you obtain skills (such as operating a HAM radio) that will be useful should a disaster strike your area.

The keys to surviving disasters are to get to a safe place immediately, remain calm and in control, and be prepared for anything. While no future event is completely predictable, the more you know about the situations that can arise, the better your chances of survival.

Once a disaster has occurred, remember to take pictures for insurance purposes. If the insurance company has before and after pictures, it will help them to process your claim more quickly and efficiently. Work together with your family and neighbors to create a sustainable survival community until damages can be repaired. Remember, people from just a couple hundred years ago were able to survive without modern day conveniences, and so can you!

www.ingramcontent.com/pod-product-compliance
Lightning Source LLC
Chambersburg PA
CBHW060418290526
45791CB00002B/805